STRATEGY *and*
ARMS CONTROL

Thomas C. Schelling

Morton H. Halperin

With the Assistance of Donald G. Brennan

Martino Publishing
Mansfield Centre, CT
2014

Martino Publishing
P.O. Box 373,
Mansfield Centre, CT 06250 USA

ISBN 978-1-61427-758-3

© *2014 Martino Publishing*

Cover design by T. Matarazzo

Printed in the United States of America On 100% Acid-Free Paper

STRATEGY *and* ARMS CONTROL

Thomas C. Schelling

Morton H. Halperin

With the Assistance of Donald G. Brennan

THE TWENTIETH CENTURY FUND

NEW YORK: 1961

THE SUMMER STUDY ON

ARMS CONTROL

OF THE AMERICAN ACADEMY

OF ARTS AND SCIENCES

Written under the auspices of

THE CENTER FOR

INTERNATIONAL AFFAIRS

HARVARD UNIVERSITY

FOREWORD

The Twentieth Century Fund, having been interested for some time in encouraging a fresh approach to arms control, was favorably impressed in the spring of 1960 by plans for a Summer Study group being developed under the auspices of the American Academy of Arts and Sciences. The Fund agreed to financial support of the project. The study sessions began in mid–June 1960 under the general direction of Bernard T. Feld of the Physics Department of the Massachusetts Institute of Technology; they continued until mid–September. A nucleus of regular participants was augmented by a number of part-time visitors and contributors. In all, some fifty persons from universities and research institutes across the country took part in the sessions at M.I.T.'s Endicott House near Boston. Of these, approximately twenty to twenty-five were present at any one time.

The group was under the general guidance of a steering committee composed of B.T. Feld, Chairman; D. G. Brennan, M.I.T.; P. M. Doty, Harvard; D. H. Frisch, M.I.T.; M. F. Millikan, M.I.T.; T. C. Schelling, Harvard; V. F. Weisskopf, M.I.T.; and J. B. Wiesner, M.I.T. After mid–September, several of the activities initiated during the summer were coordinated by D. G. Brennan. The project was terminated in January 1961.

The present volume is one of the fruits of this enterprise. Written by T. C. Schelling and M. H. Halperin at the Harvard Center for International Affairs, it presents an analysis of arms control with particular emphasis on the military policy involved. The Twentieth Century Fund is also publishing a companion volume, *Arms Reduction — Program and Issues*, edited by D. H. Frisch, a discussion of specific plans and important components of arms-control systems. In addition, there have been reproduced in limited quantities, available to those professionally interested, two by-products of the study group: (1) a collection of seminar notes, working papers and "exercises"; and (2) a short collection of papers relating to nonphysical, or "psychological," inspection techniques.

Finally, a book by Arthur Hadley, based partly on his association with the Summer Study, is scheduled for publication by the Viking Press in 1961.

The general objectives of the study were to advance some aspects of the intellectual state of the art in arms control and to provide some concrete data on a few technical and strategic problems of potential importance. We believe the several volumes will demonstrate that these objectives have been reasonably accomplished, though they leave untouched many wide areas. The study group did not arrive at a consensus on recommended policies for governmental action, but much of the material in the reports will unquestionably be of considerable value in the further evolution of national policy.

The Twentieth Century Fund is appreciative of the efforts made by a large number of individuals in bringing this project to a conclusion. It hopes that the work will be a factor in bringing the world back from its present uneasy and highly dangerous posture.

AUGUST HECKSCHER, *Director*
THE TWENTIETH CENTURY FUND

41 East 70th Street, New York
February 1961

ACKNOWLEDGMENTS

In preparing this book, and in preparing for it, we enjoyed an intensive summer of argument and education at the hands of our colleagues in the Summer Study on Arms Control. The individual participants in that enterprise are listed in the Appendix. We cannot possibly disentangle our individual debts to them; as a group they were not only stimulating and informative but directly helpful in commenting on the original outline and early drafts. We have enjoyed, too, much rough but sympathetic handling by the Harvard–M.I.T. Faculty Seminar on Arms Control. The 1960–61 Fellows of the Harvard Center for International Affairs pitched in their share of critical advice. From all this we have benefited enormously; but in the end we have tried to please nobody but ourselves.

We had the advantage of seeing a draft of Mr. Hedley Bull's forthcoming book, *The Control of the Arms Race*, prepared for the Institute for Strategic Studies; and we have benefited from the several essays to appear in Donald G. Brennan (ed.), *Arms Control, Disarmament and National Security* (George Braziller, Inc.), many of which appeared in the Fall 1960 issue of *Daedalus*. Henry N. Rowen and Fred C. Iklé gave us detailed comments and advice on the entire manuscript.

The contribution of Donald G. Brennan, in the Summer Study, in the Faculty Seminar, and in continuous direct collaboration with us, was on such a scale that the title page is the only proper place to acknowledge it.

THOMAS C. SCHELLING

MORTON H. HALPERIN

CONTENTS

CONTENTS

INTRODUCTION

THIS study is an attempt to identify the meaning of arms control in the era of modern weapons, and its role in the pursuit of national and international security. It is not an advertisement for arms control; it is as concerned with problems and difficulties, qualifications and limitations, as it is with opportunities and promises. It is an effort to fit arms control into our foreign and military policy, and to demonstrate how naturally it fits rather than how novel it is.

This is, however, a sympathetic exploration of arms control. We believe that arms control is a promising, but still only dimly perceived, enlargement of the scope of our military strategy. It rests essentially on the recognition that our military relation with potential enemies is not one of pure conflict and opposition, but involves strong elements of mutual interest in the avoidance of a war that neither side wants, in minimizing the costs and risks of the arms competition, and in curtailing the scope and violence of war in the event it occurs.

Particularly in the modern era, the purpose of military force is not simply to win wars. It is the responsibility of military force to deter aggression, while avoiding the kind of threat that may provoke desperate, preventive, or irrational military action on the part of other countries. It is the responsibility of military policies and postures to avoid the false alarms and misunderstandings that might lead to a war that both sides would deplore.

In short, while a nation's military force opposes the military force of potentially hostile nations, it also must collaborate, implicitly if not explicitly, in avoiding the kinds of crises in which withdrawal is intolerable for both sides, in avoiding false alarms and mistaken intentions, and in providing — along with its deterrent threat of resistance or retaliation in the event of unacceptable challenges — reassurance that restraint on the part of potential enemies will be matched by restraint on our own. It is the responsibility of military

1

policy to recognize that, just as our own military establishment is largely a response to the military force that confronts us, foreign military establishments are to some extent a response to our own, and there can be a mutual interest in inducing and reciprocating arms restraint.

We use the term "arms control" rather than "disarmament." Our intention is simply to broaden the term. We mean to include all the forms of military cooperation between potential enemies in the interest of reducing the likelihood of war, its scope and violence if it occurs, and the political and economic costs of being prepared for it. The essential feature of arms control is the recognition of the common interest, of the possibility of reciprocation and cooperation even between potential enemies with respect to their military establishments. Whether the most promising areas of arms control involve reductions in certain kinds of military force, increases in certain kinds of military force, qualitative changes in weaponry, different modes of deployment, or arrangements superimposed on existing military systems, we prefer to treat as an open question.

If both sides can profit from improved military communications, from more expensive military forces that are less prone to accident, from expensive redeployments that minimize the danger of misinterpretation and false alarm, arms control may cost more not less. It may by some criteria seem to involve more armament not less. If we succeed in reducing the danger of certain kinds of war, and reciprocally deny ourselves certain apparent military advantages (of the kind that cancel out for the most part if both sides take advantage of them), and if in so doing we increase our military requirements for other dangers of warfare, the matter must be judged on its merits and not simply according to whether the sizes of armies go up or down. If it appears that the danger of accidental war can be reduced by improved intelligence about each other's military doctrines and modes of deployment, or by the provision of superior communication between governments in the event of military crisis, these may have value independently of whether military forces increase, decrease, or are unaffected.

This approach is not in opposition to "disarmament" in the more literal sense, involving the straightforward notion of simple reductions in military force, military manpower, military budgets, aggregate explosive power, and so forth. It is intended rather to include such disarmament in a broader concept. We do not, however, share the notion, implicit in many pleas for disarmament, that a reduction in the level of military forces is necessarily desirable if only it is "inspectable" and that it necessarily makes war less likely. The reader will find that most of the present study is concerned less with reducing national *capabilities* for destruction in the event of war than in reducing the *incentives* that may lead to war or that may cause war to be the more destructive in the event it occurs. We are particularly concerned with those incentives that arise from the character of modern weapons and the expectations they create.

An important premise underlying the point of view of this study is that a main determinant of the likelihood of war is the nature of present military technology and present military expectations. We and the Soviets are to some extent trapped by our military technology. Weapon developments of the last fifteen years, especially of the last seven or eight, have themselves been responsible for some of the most alarming aspects of the present strategic situation. They have enhanced the advantage, in the event war should come, of being the one to start it, or of responding instantly and vigorously to evidence that war may have started. They have inhumanly compressed the time available to make the most terrible decisions. They have almost eliminated the expectation that a general war either could be or should be limited in scope or brought to a close by any process other than the sheer exhaustion of weapons on both sides. They have greatly reduced the confidence of either side that it can predict the weapons its enemy has or will have in the future. In these and other ways the evolution of military technology has exacerbated whatever propensities towards war are inherent in the political conflict between us and our potential enemies. And the greatly increased destructive power of weapons, while it may make both sides more cautious, may make the failure to control these propensities extremely costly.

Arms control can be thought of as an effort, by some kind of reciprocity or cooperation with our potential enemies, to minimize, to offset, to compensate or to deflate some of these characteristics of modern weapons and military expectations. In addition to what we can do unilaterally to improve our warning, to maintain close control over our forces, to make our forces more secure against attack, to avoid the need for precipitant decisions, to avoid accidents or the mistaken decisions that they might cause and to contain conflict once it starts, there may be opportunities to exchange facilities or understandings with our enemies, or to design and deploy our forces differently by agreement with our enemies who do likewise, in a way that enhances those aspects of technology that we like and that helps to nullify those that we do not.

We say this to anticipate the objection that armaments are only a reflection of existing conflicts and not a cause of them. It is true that modern armaments and military plans are a response to basic international conflicts. It is also true that the size and character of military forces are an important determinant of national fears and anxieties, and of the military incentives of our potential enemies. There is a feedback between our military forces and the conflicts that they simultaneously reflect and influence. We have no expectation that by working on weaponry alone, or military deployments or expectations, we can eliminate the political, economic and ideological differences that genuinely underlie present international antagonisms. We do believe that much can be done through careful design of our military strategy, our weaponry, our military deployments and doctrines, to reduce the military danger of those hostilities to our security. We believe that, in addition to what can be accomplished unilaterally in this regard, there are actions and restraints for which the inducements are greater on each side if the other side reciprocates or leads the way. And we believe that something in the way of rules, traditions, and clearer expectations about each other's reactions and modes of behavior may reduce the likelihood of military action based on mistake or misunderstanding.

What is striking is not how novel the methods and purposes of arms control are, and how different from the methods and purposes of national military policy; what is striking is how much overlap there is. There is hardly an objective of arms control to be described in this study that is not equally a continuing urgent objective of national military strategy — of our unilateral military plans and policies. What this study tries to do is to suggest those points at which these unilateral actions can be extended or supplemented through joint understandings with our potential enemies. In some cases the scope for such reciprocal action seems substantial, in other cases very modest; but in all cases it seems worth taking into consideration. Since this dimension of military policy has traditionally been so little appreciated, we have felt it worth while to indicate many areas in which arms control may possibly prove helpful, even if we cannot yet perceive just where the promise lies.

We have also considered arms control to include the less formal, less institutionalized, less "negotiated" understandings and agreements. Some may object that there is no "control" when both sides simply abstain from an action which, if done by one party, yields an advantage but if done by both parties cancels out the advantages and raises risks all around. Our resolution of this semantic problem is to interpret "control" to mean induced or reciprocated "self-control," whether the inducements include negotiated treaties or just informal understandings and reciprocated restraints.

In surveying the possible areas in which arms control may play a role, we have tried to err on the generous side, doubting whether we can yet perceive all of the forms that arms control may take and the areas in which it may occur. In our discussion of the negotiation and administration of concrete agreements, we have been concerned to identify the difficulties, in the belief that these must be anticipated if experiments at arms control are to avoid unnecessary disappointment or disaster.

We have not stated what we believe to be the "ultimate goal" of arms control — whether it be a world disarmed, a world policed by a single benevolent military force or a world in which some military "balance of prudence" has taken the fear out of the "balance of fear." We should, however, acknowledge that we do not believe the problems of war and peace and international conflict are susceptible of any once-for-all solution. Something like eternal vigilance and determination would be required to keep peace in the world at any stage of disarmament, even total disarmament. International conflict, and the military forces that are their reflection, are not in our judgment simply unnatural growths in human society which, once removed, need never recur. Conflict of interest is a social phenomenon unlikely to disappear, and potential recourse to violence and damage will always suggest itself if the conflict gets out of hand. Man's capability for self-destruction cannot be eradicated — he knows too much! Keeping that capability under control — providing incentives to minimize recourse to violence — is the eternal challenge.

This is the objective of responsible military policy. And a conscious adjustment of our military forces and policies to take account of those of our potential enemies, in the common interest of restraining violence, is what we mean by arms control.

In the study that follows we are concerned mainly with the direct relation of arms control to the military environment. Arms control can also affect, for good or ill, our political relations with allies, neutrals and potential enemies. It can reduce tension or hostilities; it can reduce vigilance. It can strengthen alliances, collapse them, or make them unnecessary. It can create confidence and trust or create suspicion and irritation. It can lead to greater world organization and the rule of law or discredit them. And it evidently lends itself to the short-run competition in propaganda.

In focusing this book on the military environment we have not meant to depreciate the more purely political and psychological consequences. We have just not covered the whole subject. We do, however, incline to the view that the political and psychological benefits that may stem from arms control will be the more genuine, the more genuine is the direct contribution to international security. We doubt therefore whether the approach of this book is wholly inconsistent with an approach that emphasizes the political environment more and the military environment less.

In Part I we explore the potential contributions of arms control to the military environment. "Potential" needs emphasis. It is easy to see, under most of the headings in Part I, that some kind of formal or informal arms control could in theory help in the solution of our security problems. It is quite another matter to identify important, feasible applications of the principle. We have included illustrative suggestions, but have no comprehensive scheme to propose.

And we particularly emphasize that there may be more, much more, to be accomplished under many of the headings of Part I by unilateral improvements in our military policies and posture than through the medium of arms control. It is not true that an improvement in our military posture is necessarily a disadvantage to a potential enemy. The right kind of "improvement" can reduce the danger that a potential enemy will become an active one, and can lay the groundwork for deflating the enmity itself.

Part I is concerned with potential benefits. Problems and difficulties, risks and uncertainties, receive attention in Parts II and III.

PART I

THE POTENTIAL SECURITY FUNCTIONS OF ARMS CONTROL

Chapter 1

ARMS CONTROL
AND GENERAL WAR

THE most mischievous character of today's strategic weapons is that they may provide an enormous advantage, in the event that war occurs, to the side that starts it. Both Russian and American strategic doctrines reflect preoccupation with the urgency of attacking in the event of evidence that the other is about to. The urgency is in the vulnerability of strategic weapons themselves, and of the communication and other facilities they depend on; the side that attacks first can hope to blunt the other's retaliation. Closely related is the advantage, in the event the other is already attacking, of responding quickly and vigorously — of being a close second if not first.

By itself this urgency would pose the danger of unintended war, a war provoked by ambiguous evidence of attack. The greater the urgency with which the decision must be made in the event of alarm, the greater the likelihood of converting a false alarm into war itself. These dangers compound themselves: each side must be alert not only to the other's premeditated attack, but to the other's incentive to reach quick decisions in an emergency.

Hardly any other characteristic of weapons dramatizes so well that some of the danger of war resides in the very character of modern weapons. Hardly anything would be as tragically ironic as a war that both sides started, each in the belief that the other was about to, each compelled by its expectations to confirm the other's belief that attack was imminent.

This danger does not depend on the belief that by striking

9

quickly one may come off with a clean win. The comparison is not between initiating war and no war at all, but between initiating war and waiting for the other to initiate it. It may not be optimism that provides the dangerous incentive, but pessimism about the loss from failing to act in time. It is essentially "preventive war," improvised at a moment when war is considered imminent. *Preemptive* war is the term now in use for the case of war initiated in the expectation that attack is imminent.

At no time before in modern history did military technology make it so likely that the first moments of general war might determine its outcome. Whatever the Japanese expected from Pearl Harbor, it would have been a mistake to believe that they could foreclose an American victory by anything they might accomplish that one morning. In World War I, when nations were caught in the ponderous grip of mobilization procedures that provided advantage to the side that first started to mobilize, there may have been a slow-motion equivalent to nuclear attack. But in 1914 the difference between mobilizing half a day before the enemy and half a day behind was on a different scale of importance.*

THE INCENTIVE TO PRE-EMPT

There are several ways that arms control might possibly help. One is to alter the character of the weapons themselves, especially their vulnerability to each other — their potency in foreclosing return attack. Whatever reduces the ability of weapons to achieve advantage by going quickly, and to suffer a great disadvantage by responding slowly, may reduce the likelihood of war.

A second approach is oriented towards the events that might precipitate pre-emptive decisions. Essentially, the urge to pre-empt

* For a discussion of vulnerability in relation to the strategic balance see Bernard Brodie, *Strategy in the Missile Age* (Princeton: Princeton University Press, 1959); Herman Kahn, *On Thermonuclear War* (Princeton: Princeton University Press, 1960); Washington Center for Foreign Policy Research, *Developments in Military Technology and Their Impact on United States Strategy and Foreign Policy*, Study No. 8, December 1959, prepared for the Senate Committee on Foreign Relations, 86th Congress, 2d Session (Washington: U.S. Government Printing Office, 1959); Albert Wohlstetter, "The Delicate Balance of Terror," *Foreign Affairs* XXXVII (January 1959) 211–34 and his forthcoming book. For an analysis of the problem in the arms-control context see Thomas C. Schelling, "Surprise Attack and Disarmament," in *The Strategy of Conflict* (Cambridge: Harvard University Press, 1960) 230–54.

is an *aggravating* factor: it converts a possibility of war into an anticipation of war, precipitating war. The pre-emptive advantage makes a suspicion of war a cause of war. If the actions, false alarms, accidental events, mischief or other occurrences that bring the pre-emptive urge into play can be minimized and damped, by co-operative arrangements or arms limitations, the danger of pre-emptive war may be reduced.

Third, arms control may possibly address itself to the decision process, and particularly to the expectations of each side about the other's actions or intentions on the brink of war. If cooperative ar-rangements can improve each side's intelligence about the other's preparatory actions, this may (but also may not) stabilize expecta-tions. If each is able to reassure the other that it is not misinterpret-ing certain events as signalling the onset of war, dangerously com-pounding expectations may be averted. If each can avoid, in responding to the enhanced danger of war, actions and deploy-ments that appear as preparations for attack, and can enhance the other's ability to perceive this, the interacting decisions that might explode into war may be damped.

Finally, it is likely that any forms of arms control that reduce the general expectation of war would reduce the urgency to pre-empt and the fear of each other's obsession with pre-emption.

THE INCENTIVE FOR
PREMEDITATED ATTACK

As far as major war is concerned, the incentive to initiate a pre-meditated attack is akin to the incentive towards pre-emptive at-tack. The reason is that with thermonuclear weapons on both sides, there might be little inducement in either case if it were not for the possibility of achieving, by taking the initiative, a substantial re-duction in the other's ability or willingness to retaliate.

What creates the principal danger of premeditated attack is the same as with pre-emptive attack: the vulnerability of either side's retaliatory forces to an attack by the other. With a technology that permits an enormously potent weapon to arrive on an enemy target in a matter of minutes, the possibility is open that a well-coordi-nated surprise attack on the other side's own strategic forces might greatly reduce the size of these forces. By disrupting communica-tions and disorganizing the victim's forces, the attacker can reduce the efficiency even of the weapons surviving; and they would have to be used against an attacker whose own defenses had the advantage of alertness and preparation. There is also the possibility that an attacker might hope to disarm the victim sufficiently to make retaliation appear futile.

Thus premeditated strategic attack by one major power against the other is largely a matter of the advantage of initiative and surprise. Collaborative measures to reduce this advantage, and to reduce thereby the incentive that either might have towards premeditated attack, might be an important supplement to the measures that we undertake unilaterally to assure our strategic forces against attack.

First, there may be measures that, taken jointly, would reduce the likelihood that the attacker could achieve *surprise*. Exchange of warning and intelligence facilities would be an example; and the original "open-skies" idea was oriented this way. In addition to warning arrangements, there might be limitations on weapons themselves, or on their use and deployment, designed to reduce their *capability for achieving surprise*. Limitations on the basing of weapons, or a requirement that they show up and be counted, might be of this sort. In other words, cooperative measures to improve intelligence and warning facilities, or cooperative measures with respect to weapons themselves designed to facilitate warning, might be considered.

Second, measures might be considered that would make weapons *less vulnerable even in the event of surprise*. Agreement to develop and to acquire weapons of a character relatively better for retaliation than for achieving surprise (as might have been the case if it had been possible to limit the accuracy of missiles) might reduce the incentives on both sides for initiating general war. Alternatively, since the advantage in striking first is largely in reducing or precluding a punitive return attack, measures to defend the homeland against incoming punitive weapons are complementary to offensive weapons of surprise attack. Thus abstention from active defense of cities (or, conceivably, from civil defense preparations) might increase the potency of each side's retaliatory forces in a manner analogous to the protection of the retaliatory forces themselves.

It has to be asked whether there is not some logical contradiction in both sides' wishing to eliminate the advantages that go with premeditated attack. Either one side is in fact interested in carrying out a well-coordinated attack on the other's strategic forces, or else not. If not, the measures appear superfluous. If so, there is at least one partner who is against the purpose of the agreement, and who either would not enter it or would do so only if he were certain that he could subvert it. Can there be a mutual interest in measures to frustrate premeditated attack?

For several reasons the answer can be "yes." It may be that neither side intends to attack but is uneasy about the other's intentions. It is thus obliged to develop military forces and to deploy them in a way that assumes the other side *may* attack; and it is obliged to react to ambiguous events as though the other side would indeed attack. If, then, neither in fact intends deliberate attack, there could be a good deal to gain by creating for both sides the reassurance that may accompany measures jointly taken to reduce the likelihood that either side, if it attacked, would succeed. In other words, since estimates of each other's *intentions* will necessarily be uncertain, measures reciprocally to reduce *capabilities* for preclusive attack may help both.

Second, even though neither side presently considers it wise or necessary to initiate general war, political events or technological change may alter the situation. But it may change either way: *either* we *or* the Russians may be the victim or beneficiary of technological break-through, of moments of military weakness, or of political incentives that override the fear of general war. Each of us may well be willing to relinquish capabilities in future contingencies on condition that the other side do likewise. (If a flip of a coin might give either of us the capability for successful attack it could look like a bad bet to both of us.)

Third, a main incentive — perhaps the overwhelmingly important motivation — towards premeditated attack on the other side's strategic forces would be a belief that war, sooner or later, is fairly likely, and that the *conservative* course would be to initiate it on the best possible terms. So-called "preventive war" considerations may be uppermost. This, in effect, is the "pre-emptive" urge in slow motion. The pre-emptive motive is the incentive to attack in the belief that the other is already attacking or is about to; the "preventive urge" has the same forestalling motives, but with respect to a war that is not yet imminent.

But the "preventive" and the "pre-emptive" urges can interact dangerously. The greater the "preventive urge" that either imputes to the other, the more probable it must expect an attack to be. The more alert it must itself then be to the need for a pre-emptive decision.

Furthermore, the preventive urges on both sides compound with each other. A powerful reason why one side might decide that a planned "preventive" attack was the only prudent action would be a belief that the other would sooner or later reach the same conclusion. The danger might be substantially deflated by measures that reduced the likely success of attack, by reducing both sides' *expectations* of attack.

THE DANGER OF ACCIDENTAL WAR

In current usage "accidental war" refers to a war that, in some sense, neither side intended, expected or deliberately prepared for. It includes war that might result from errors in warning systems or misinterpretations of tactical evidence. It includes the notion that a literal accident, such as the inadvertent detonation of a nuclear weapon, might precipitate war through misinterpretation, through expectation of the enemy's misinterpretation or through some sequence of automatic or semiautomatic responses and decisions. It includes the possibility of unauthorized provocative action by a pilot or bomber or missile commander; sabotage that inadvertently goes beyond its limited objectives; and plain mischief with or without the intended consequence of war. And it has come to include what is sometimes called "catalytic war" — a deliberate plot by some third country or countries, perhaps with nuclear weapons, to precipitate a war between the major powers (or just to precipitate a crisis, but with the consequence of war).*

"Accidental war" is sometimes used also to refer to mistakes in "brinkmanship," failure to foresee the consequences of military actions, or the accumulation of irreversible threats in the heat of a

---

* For a discussion of accidental war see Thomas C. Schelling, "Meteors, Mischief, and War," *Bulletin of the Atomic Scientists* XVI (September 1960) 292–97; John B. Phelps *et al.*, *Accidental War: Some Dangers in the 1960's,* RP-6, The Mershon National Security Program, The Ohio State University, June 29, 1960.

crisis. And it may refer to the particular occurrences or misunderstandings by which limited war explodes into general war.

The essential character of accidental war is that of a war initiated in the belief that war has already started or become inevitable. In most of the hypothetical cases of "accidental war," evidence is misread by one or both sides. (There is an important qualification: if both sides jump to the conclusion that instant war is inevitable, both sides may immediately make this conclusion "correct.")

It would not be accidents themselves, ambiguous spots on a radarscope, the mischief of a deranged bomber pilot, the sabotage, or the catalytic actions of third parties, that would *directly* bring about war. These occurrences provoke *decisions* that bring about war. The problem, therefore, is not solely one of preventing the "accidents"; it is equally, or more, one of forestalling the kinds of *decisions* that might lead to war as a result of accident, false alarm or mischief.

This idea of "accidental war" rests largely on the same premise that underlies pre-emptive war — that there is an enormous advantage, in the event war occurs, in starting it (or enormous advantage, in the event it seems to have started, in responding instantly) and that each side will be not only conscious of this but conscious of the other's preoccupation with it. It seems quite unlikely that war would be brought about by an electronic false alarm, by a mechanical accident, by the mischief of someone in a message center or on an airbase or by the provocative action of a third party, if there were not some urgency of responding before the evidence is in. The essence of a false alarm is that, if one fails to act upon it, it is seen to have been a false alarm. An accident is almost certain to be recognized as an accident, if war has not intervened meanwhile. And among all those who may have it in their power to bring about a provocative event that might precipitate the decisions that bring about war, very few, if any, would have the power to wage a persuasive imitation of war if the consequences of their actions could be assessed and analyzed for even a brief period of time. Thus "accidental war" is war that may be initiated on misinformation, incomplete evidence or misunderstanding, of a kind that could likely be cleared up were it not that the time to clear it up might seem a disastrous delay to a government confronted with the possibility that war has already started. "Accidental war" is, for the most part, pre-emptive war sparked by some occurrence that was unpredictable, outside the control of the main participants and unintended by them.

There are several ways that arms control might possibly help to reduce the danger of accidental war. An important one has been mentioned: reducing the urgency of quick action at the outset of general war. Cooperative or unilateral measures to improve the ability of each side's strategic forces to survive an attack, *and to remain under good command and control under attack,* might slow down the tempo of decisions. Slowing down decisions on the brink of war not only means that either side, if it wishes to, can take more time to clear up whether or not the war has already started; it also means that each can impute less impetuous action to the other, and reduce thereby the need for its own quick reaction.

Measures to reduce the incidence of false alarm could be helpful. Exchange of warning facilities, of facilities for last-minute tactical intelligence, might reduce the incidence of false alarms by increasing the reliability of the warning system and improving the flow of evidence to each side. (Increased warning facilities might also increase the false-alarm rate; and some superficially attractive schemes for mutual warning probably could not communicate rapidly enough to be of use within the relevant span of time.) Agreements to limit the kinds of activities and deployments that might create misunderstandings or false alarms could also be helpful; even arrangements or activities that just improved each side's understanding of the other's behavior, facilitating discrimination between normal and abnormal traffic, might help.

And because the essence of this accidental-war problem is misunderstanding on one side or both, it is not out of the question that communications and other arrangements might be set up to facilitate direct contact between governments, of a sort that could clear up misunderstandings and provide certain assurances in an emergency. (The possibility that such arrangements could be abused is discussed later. Here — as emphasized — we are exploring the potential advantages of arms arrangements; the qualifications and disadvantages will appear in Parts II and III.)

Finally, to the extent that arms control helps to limit local war, or can reduce American and Soviet expectations of general war, the less likely it is that accidental occurrences will be construed as evidence of war.

CAPABILITIES FOR DESTRUCTION

Arms limitations might reduce the capability for destruction so that, in the event of a thermonuclear American-Soviet exchange, no matter how the war gets out of hand, the damage is less than it would have been otherwise. The main form such an agreement might take is to reduce existing nuclear stock piles or the capability for delivering them. No agreement can erase the knowledge of how to produce nuclear weapons and long-range missiles; an agreement could, however, aim at reducing the amount of fissionable material or the vehicles for their delivery. The capability for instantaneous destruction might thus be lowered, and the likelihood increased that war would come to an end within the time it would take to increase nuclear stockpiles or delivery systems. Acceptance of reduced nuclear stockpiles and vehicles would imply acceptance of the notion that something less than unlimited supplies of nuclear weapons and missiles may be adequate to deter attack. It could also reflect a belief that retaliatory forces might not be much degraded, if at all, if both they *and* the attacking force were comparably diminished. Also, since small nuclear weapons can fairly easily and quickly be converted into large weapons, any agreement to reduce substantially the nuclear stockpile, and hence the capability for destruction in general war, might require some willingness on both sides to reduce their dependence on nuclear weapons in limited warfare. (A missile agreement in itself might not be very effective in reducing over-all capability for destruction — in contrast to capability for, e.g., surprise attack — because bombers can carry much greater loads than contemporary missiles.)

Any agreement that reduced the capability for destruction in general war might make war more likely, in that the costs and risks in initiating it would not appear as great.

It should be noted that since both the Soviet Union and the United States now produce large quantities of nuclear weapons, and presumably will continue in the absence of any agreement to cut off production, such an agreement could have some effect of reducing future capability for destruction in general war, whether or not there was an agreement to reduce previously existing stock-piles.

A most important possibility is that the over-all level of potential destruction might be substantially reduced by arms arrangements that did not focus on numbers and sizes of weapons *per se*. If both Soviet and American forces should succeed, through cooperative measures or unilaterally, in developing reasonably invulnerable retaliatory systems, so that neither could disarm the other in a sudden attack and neither needed to be obsessed with the imminence of attack, a large reduction in numbers might come naturally. Certainly, nothing like the nuclear-energy delivery capability of our present bomber force would be needed if the entire force were reasonably secure against attack and if Soviet forces were similarly secure against our attack. Insurance in *numbers* against enemy surprise attack would be less needed if security were achieved qualitatively. Furthermore, the kinds of forces that would maximize *retaliatory* capability, in contrast to pre-emptive capability, and that would permit the most deliberate and controlled response to alarms and accidents, could prove to be quite expensive in relation to explosive energy. A weapon system, or mix of weapons, that maximizes the explosive power it could deliver to targets *after* being attacked is likely to involve a much smaller aggregate warhead yield (per dollar expended on it) than a force designed to profit from a pre-emptive attack.

Thus an appreciable quantitative "disarmament" may result as a natural by-product of qualitative changes in strategic armaments.

COLLATERAL DAMAGE

It seems to be widely thought that a war between the U.S. and the U.S.S.R. would necessarily be an "all-out" affair, motivated towards maximum destruction of each other. In contrast to so-called "limited war," general war is seen as a wholly indiscriminate and unrestrained orgy of punitive action. To some extent, this belief is cultivated by a deterrent strategy that feels obliged to make the threat of war as awful as possible (or by a strategy of intimidation that aims at the same thing). Both American and Soviet expressed doctrine has often implied that "limited war" is local war and occupies some range at the lower end of the scale, while "general war" must be total.

It is not evident that this would be the case. Whatever the tragedy and damage that one should anticipate in the event of war, it is not at all clear that a strategic war between the U.S. and the U.S.S.R. would necessarily be motivated towards maximum destruction. Particularly as we consider an "accidental" or pre-emptively motivated war, one that the initiator himself deplores, one that is "self-defensive," or one that results from the piling up of threatening commitments on both sides from which no retreat seems possible, we have to consider a war that would be aimed less at punitive destruction and more at the survival of each country and its further military security. Furthermore, even if a nation tries to deter or to intimidate the other with a threat that any war, once it passes some threshold, will know no bounds, the government's actual motivation if war occurs would not — if any rationality at all remains and if command arrangements are adequately designed — be towards fulfilling a threat that had failed. It would instead be motivated towards maximizing the nation's security and other interests.

If this is so, there are at least two considerations suggesting that general war might be less destructive than is generally thought. One is that the highest priority targets would be retaliatory forces, not populations and economic assets. A cold-blooded war plan might have antipopulation measures low on its list of objectives.

The second consideration is that an attacker might deliberately abstain from destroying population centers, if those population centers did not contain high priority strategic targets, in the hope of deterring the all-out destruction of his own cities and bringing the war to a close. "General war" might also be "limited war." The attacker might consider it in his interest to avoid cities because alive they represent hostages with which he can bargain. He could use the *threat* of further destruction in bargaining for a termination of the war, perhaps a termination that included subsequent arms control. The attacked country might be similarly alert to the possibility of defending cities not through active measures but through coercion, through preserving the *threat* of destroying the attacker's cities. Whether one or both sides abstain altogether from population targets, or engage in limited "negotiatory" blows at population centers, there is at least some reason to suppose that the deliberate military action would be somewhat confined to urgent military targets.

If this is a possibility — if the attacker either cannot afford to waste weapons on population strikes, or prefers to exploit the *threat* of further destruction rather than to destroy potential hostages at the outset — there remains the important question whether it is physically possible. Might cities and populations be destroyed as a by-product of a war that, in so far as deliberate military action is concerned, is aimed at "military" targets? Might arms limitations, or reciprocal modifications in arms programs, or *understandings about the conduct of war,* reduce the collateral damage (by-product damage) of a war confined as far as possible to military engagements?

The issue of clean and dirty bombs comes immediately to mind. Similarly important is the location of strategic weapons; if they are located away from cities, and if strategic communications are independent of city communications, there may be little blast damage to major population centers, at least from weapons that do not go astray. If weapons and related facilities (i.e., if the prime targets) can be isolated from population centers, the fallout can be reduced and its arrival retarded.

Efforts along these lines would likely be unilateral rather than collaborative. Nevertheless, any comprehensive understanding that specifies the *kinds* of strategic weapons that each side should have ought to take into consideration the desirability of weapons that need not destroy cities and populations unless deliberately aimed at them, or that do not, by their location, make urgent targets out of population centers.

There is admittedly a dilemma. An important objective of arms control may be to permit each side a reasonably potent retaliatory force — a force that could do acute punitive damage to the other side's population and other values. If so, it might seem a contradiction of purpose to "sanitize" a weapon system in such a way as to remove its retaliatory potential. Indeed this would be true of measures designed to make retaliatory weapons *incapable* of retaliation. What is being suggested here is much more modest — the possibility of leaving an *option* to the possessor of the weapons, so that while he has a capability for retaliation he need not create enormous destruction as a by-product of a pre-emptive or an "accidental" war initiated by one side or the other in a manner designed to minimize damage. True, the threat of retaliation may be deflated by anything that leaves the deterrent force the option of restraining itself. Nevertheless, there is a possibility here that deserves consideration even though the arguments go both ways. (To the extent that damage to third areas — noncombatants in the war — would be affected, the retaliatory dilemma does not arise.)

It is interesting that *types* of weapons often involve *locational* questions. A main difference between Polaris submarines and the fixed-base ICBM's is that the former spend most of their time away from population centers, while the latter tend to be within national boundaries and, depending on geographical considerations, perhaps quite close to populations. Thus an important issue in the question whether arms control should promote or suppress, say, ballistic-missile submarines, is the implication for collateral damage in a pre-emptively motivated war.

And here it is clear that there may be a difference between a retaliatory system that achieves invulnerability by requiring a large number of attacking weapons to destroy it, and one that achieves invulnerability by providing no useful target to the enemy. In the event a military duel should get started, digging up each other's missiles by exploding large warheads on each other's territory creates enormous amounts of fallout; *searching* for hidden or mobile missiles does not. Blanketing an area known to contain weapons whose exact location is not known, on the other hand, can involve large amounts of fallout. And so on. Collateral damage to earthbound population and structures may even depend on whether the violent attempts to destroy each other's retaliatory forces are out in space.

THE INCENTIVE FOR DESTRUCTION

We have just discussed the possibility that arms control might help to limit damage in general war in the event both sides wish to limit damage. It may also concern itself with reducing the incentive for destruction in case of war.

One possibility is to create *expectations* that even a major strategic war might be susceptible of limitation. The main motivation for restraint would be to induce reciprocation; the likelihood of its being reciprocated depends on the other side's being alert to the possibility of restraint, being able to recognize restraint if it occurs, and having some capability for responding to it. Creating a shared expectation of the possibility may therefore be a prerequisite to restraint; and any understandings, even tacit ones, that can be reached, however informal they are, deserve to be considered.

Being able to observe and to respond to restraint depends on more, however. The nature of the restraint must be recognizable; it must form some kind of pattern that the other side can recognize and respond to. There must also be some sensation of appropriateness about the restraints observed. Limits are more likely to be stable, to be appreciated by both sides as a common expectation, if they meet certain psychological and legalistic requirements, and have some rationality. A certain amount of communication, even inadvertent communication and communication of a quite informal sort, may prepare the ground for some common notion of what restraints it would be sensible to observe in the course of war. If the two sides' anticipations differ too greatly, it may be impossible to strike a "bargain" in the process of war.

Each side must furthermore have some reconnaissance and intelligence capability for knowing what is going on in the course of war — knowing a good deal more than would be required just to fight a war of extermination and exhaustion. In fighting an "all-out" war, a war of sheer destructive fury, it may make little difference to the conduct of one's offensive efforts whether particular cities of his own have yet been hit by the enemy or not; but in fighting a restrained war, in knowing whether one's own abstention has been reciprocated, and in knowing what limits the enemy is proposing by his conspicuous observance of them, one must know enough of what the enemy is doing to appreciate what his expectations are.

It may be worth considering whether direct communication between enemies in the course of war would help in arriving at restraints. It is by no means obvious that direct communication helps rather than hinders even where there is a will to use it and a desire to observe restraints; but the possibility is an important one and needs to be considered. Certainly the preparation of facilities and procedures for communication, if communication is deemed desirable, may require some overt cooperative preparation between enemies.

It is interesting that cooperation between potential enemies in reaching agreed limits and restraints in case of war may be less dependent on any "outcome" of negotiations than simply on the negotiations themselves. "Negotiations" may be too strong a word here, since the pertinent communications need not be formalized, institutionalized, or even recognized as negotiation. In reaching some expectation shared with the enemy about conduct in wartime it is the *understanding* that matters, not the instrument (if any) in which the understanding is expressed. For that reason, one side alone, or even a third party, might influence each side's anticipations about the conduct of war; power of *suggestion* is an important part of the process. The problem is one of creating an awareness of certain possibilities, and an understanding of how to take advantage of them in the event of war.

THE TERMINATION OF WAR

Terminating a war through anything other than just the exhaustion of weapons requires some form of arms control. Even surrender of one side to the other would require something analogous to arms control for policing the terms imposed by the victor and any conditions exacted by the surrendering side. Actually, surrender may be a poor term for the termination of thermonuclear war: anywhere between the two extremes of unconditional surrender by one side or another, the truce or other arrangements for bringing the war to a close would almost certainly require some direct communication between governments, an understanding about the disposition of weapons, and some capability for monitoring the agreement reached — the latter likely involving a substantial exchange of facilities subject to various safeguards. Each may have to police the other with vehicles that are themselves sufficiently under surveillance to preclude double cross.

Studies of arms control rarely consider the case that war has already started. Nevertheless, the kind of arms control required for terminating a war will depend on an awareness of the problem and some exploration of its implications *beforehand;* and it will require communications, reconnaissance, and command responsibilities that differ from those required for prosecuting unconditional total war. Prospects for success may be improved by any coordinated understanding reached between enemies beforehand.

This and the preceding section may seem a little unrealistic. It is not obvious that the necessary sophistication, self-control, control over the military forces, intelligence, reconnaissance, and imaginative thinking and bargaining, will be available. However, bargaining and communication between enemies might be plausible under some circumstances of general war. A war resulting from some military crisis, whether triggered by an "accidental" event or just by an irresistible urge to pre-empt, or arising out of a limited war, is likely to be one in which the opposing governments are already in communication. If the war itself is preceded by ultimata and other last minute threats and proposals, bargaining in general war might be a continuation of bargaining already in process.

This depends, of course, on the existence of facilities for wartime communication, and may depend on each side's decision not to destroy the other's communication facilities. But at least there is some reason to suppose that communication between enemies under the circumstances of general war might be a continuation of a brink-of-war state, not a complete innovation.

Chapter 2

ARMS CONTROL,
CRISES AND LIMITED WAR

I_N a speech on February 18, 1960, Secretary of
State Christian Herter pointed out that "observers might prove
useful, during a major crisis, helping to verify that neither side was
preparing a surprise attack upon the other." He went on to say that
"other arrangements for exchanging information might be developed to assure against potentially dangerous misunderstandings
about events in outer space." It has been mentioned that exchange
of warning and intelligence facilities might reduce the danger of
accidental war, might help to avoid unstable expectations leading
to pre-emptive attack. There is also the possibility of facilities, procedures, and communication between governments designed to
tranquilize crises and to provide assurances about each side's behavior. In the event of an accident, for example, it could be extremely important for each side to reassure itself that the other
recognized that it had been an accident; there may be scope, too,
for joint procedures to verify whether it was an accident and what
kind of accident it was.

MILITARY RELAXATION IN CRISES

If an emergency arises, and both sides get into an extraordinary
state of alert, recognizing themselves on the brink of war, there may
be a serious problem of working out a synchronized military relaxation.* Neither will wish to relax first, since the other is poised for

* For a discussion of crisis arms control and one possible measure, see
Thomas C. Schelling, "Arms Control: Proposal for a Special Surveillance
Force," *World Politics* XIII (October 1960) 1–18.

25

attack (even though his motive be defensive). Furthermore, a posture of extraordinary alert is the one in which misunderstandings, false alarms and military accidents are more likely to happen and to precipitate hasty decisions.

Facilities for quick negotiation of synchronized military relaxation could be important. This would require communication facilities between governments, and probably advance positioning of observers and surveillance equipment to monitor whatever temporary understanding might be reached at the peak of a crisis. This is a matter of synchronized withdrawal from the brink of war, but with the literal meaning of "withdrawal" being some reduction in alert status on both sides — at least, reduction of those forms of alert that especially enhance the capability for preclusive attack as distinct from preserving the capability to retaliate.

It could well be that an emergency got both sides into an extremely precarious alert status, that the original source of emergency subsided and that both sides were trapped in unstable positions, each unwilling to relax first, each unable to maintain its posture indefinitely. There could be motivation for each to submit temporarily to some extraordinary surveillance procedures, of a sort that might not be tolerable in perpetuity, each doing so on the condition that the other do likewise.

Anticipating emergencies and how they would arise, and predicting the status of forces on both sides, is beset by uncertainty. Nevertheless, it may be possible to create some adaptable, flexible facilities and personnel, to monitor short-term arms limitations and to facilitate negotiations to that end. Improvising such emergency limitations on the status and deployment of forces might be impossible just on account of the time required to think, communicate and move personnel and equipment, unless there had been advance planning on one side or both, and perhaps unless there had been some concerting of ideas between the two sides in advance, about who communicates with whom and what might be tolerable limitations to submit to.

THE TEMPO OF DECISIONS

Modern technology has spectacularly increased the amount of war that can be waged within a week, a day, an hour or a few minutes. The state of a war, or the state of the world, can change drastically within the time it takes to assemble people in a room and brief them on what the situation was just before they sat down. But the human ability to assimilate knowledge, to reflect on it and to reach intelligent decisions, though perhaps greatly improved, has not been improved commensurately with the acceleration of the tempo of war itself. Despite modern communications and electronic data processing, officials are still limited by ordinary human intelligence, the conventional speed of spoken language, reading motions of the eye and the emotional accompaniments of responsibility in a crisis.

The final weeks, and especially days, before the declarations of war in 1914 showed that with the decision procedures and communications of that era, governments were incapable of seeing their way and talking their way out of a war that was neither intended nor desired by any major participant. Communications, and probably the machinery of government decisions, have greatly improved since then — but not in proportion to the difference between megatonmiles per hour deliverable today by missiles with nuclear warheads and deliverable by horse-drawn artillery in 1914.

The most dangerous aspects of modern weapons, such as the pre-emptive advantage, are aggravated by the urgency of decision. Part of the difficulty is the sheer inability of organized decisions, reconnaissance, and communications to keep up with events. Both in limited war and on the brink of general war — and even (especially!) in general war itself — both sides ought to wish that the sequence of events in modern warfare could be slowed down.

Many weapon limitations seem to be oriented, implicitly if not explicitly, towards the tempo of decision. It has been suggested that keeping nuclear weapons out of limited war may help to make it possible for rational decisions to keep up with events. It has also been suggested that a ban on missiles might be evaluated partly in terms of the desirability of making strategic warfare a matter of hours again, rather than of quarter-hours or minutes. Suggestions for having missiles not in a state of readiness, for having warheads separate from them, for not having bombers at advance staging bases, for keeping ballistic-missile submarines near one's own shores, have sometimes been argued in terms of the time that would elapse between the first observable steps towards the initiation of the war and the last moment in which war might be averted.

Partly these measures have been designed to guarantee the receipt of timely warning, anticipation of which may deter the attack itself. But it has also been argued that to make the initiation of war take 24 hours longer might provide 24 hours for some kind of negotiation or investigation of misunderstandings.

Much the same can be said of various more drastic disarmament schemes. Disarmament may indeed be followed by rearmament; a war initiated with inefficient weapons on hand may become "modernized" as both sides assemble stockpiled components into usable weapons of great violence. But even to slow the pace of destruction may mean that negotiations and decisions have a better chance of halting events than if all the steps of rearmament and warfare were compressed into the shortest period.

LOCAL WARS

It is widely thought that general war is sufficiently costly to both major powers that there is a clear common interest in measures to make it less likely, particularly in measures to make an unpremeditated general war less likely. Limited war involving the major powers, however, is less obviously something that neither side can "win." There are, however, important possibilities of major-power limited war that it might be in the joint interest to reduce through measures taken jointly. If limited war might be started by an "accident," measures to avoid incidents would be helpful. If particular members of the major power blocs might initiate limited war that would drag the major powers in, measures to restrain allies of the major powers might be jointly undertaken. If the mere existence of military forces in particular areas increases the likelihood of both sides' getting committed to military action they both deplored, measures of synchronized withdrawal might be helpful. (In general, the concept of "disengagement" reflects this notion.)

Since this book is mainly concerned with those kinds of arms control that do not involve deliberate and recognizable major political settlements, measures like disengagement in Europe, joint neutralization of particular countries, boundary settlements and so forth, are not being discussed, although clearly an element of arms control is involved.

It should be noted, however, that at least some of the earlier discussions of "open skies" inspection arrangements, and the discussion of inspection zones in the middle 1950's, can be interpreted as concerned with limited-war surprise attacks, and were not necessarily bound up with new political arrangements.

The major powers have an interest also in preventing local wars among minor uncommitted nations. A number of motives might lead the United States and the Soviet Union to take measures to prevent local wars. One goal of American policy is certainly to prevent war and bloodshed anywhere. But in the thermonuclear age both sides are interested in preventing local wars that may pull them in and lead ultimately to total war. (Scenarios for accidental war often begin with a local small-power war.) Both major powers may also want to reduce the ability of third countries to bargain east against west; measures that reduce local military capacities, or quarantine local military action, may reduce the danger of local wars.

Measures to prevent local wars might take a number of forms, both formal and informal. A joint arms embargo to a particular region might result from a policy announced by one side of not shipping arms if the other does not; or alternatively by an international treaty. Arms embargoes may relate to particular countries (Laos) or continents (Africa). They may deal with all war materials or just certain weapons. One of the functions of an agreement not to supply nuclear weapons to third countries would be to reduce the danger in local wars. "Arms embargo" might also take the form of agreeing not to supply military assistance to particular countries. Agreements by the major powers not to ally themselves with particular countries or factions may occasionally serve to quarantine an area, reducing the danger both of war and of war's spreading.

Arms control aimed at preventing local wars might prove to be more easily carried out than arrangements dealing directly with the great-power balance. Cooperation in this area can more easily be informal and produces less difficult inspection and regulation problems; in addition the joint interest may be easier to perceive.

THE LIMITATION OF LOCAL WAR

Limited war is by its nature a form of arms control in that both sides cooperate to refrain from certain military actions. Certain military actions are not taken specifically because of the anticipated response from the other side. Agreements, understanding or restraints dealing with limited war might be negotiated either in peacetime or during the war; they might involve arrangements to be put into effect before the war or after war breaks out.

There are two aspects to keeping a local war limited. One is to maintain enough stability in the strategic balance so that neither side feels compelled or tempted to initiate general war. The other is to arrive at the limits that form the boundary conditions of the war. During a limited war the stability of the strategic balance is put to severe test. At such times because of the fighting, increased tensions and increased distrust, there is increased likelihood of a decision to pre-empt. In the course of a limited war, one or both sides can come to feel that total war has become so likely that it should be considered virtually inevitable; in such a condition one or the other side might decide to take the initiative while it could.

Accidental occurrences of various kinds are also more likely during a limited war and the tensions that would go with it. Thus agreements that reduce the incentive to pre-empt, the incentive to premeditated attack, and the danger of accidental war, would all serve to help keep local wars limited, because of the contribution that they would make to the stability of the strategic balance.

Arms understandings can also contribute to keeping local wars limited by facilitating the process of arriving at limits under which the war will be fought. The process of limiting war requires either explicit or tacit bargaining, and arms understandings reached before a war may facilitate this process. Prewar arrangements might simply involve a U.S.–Soviet discussion — formal or, more likely, very informal — of the nature of limited war. Such communication of views might help to make it clear to each side that the other accepted the notion of the limited use of force in the nuclear-missile age. It could mean that if a limited war did break out neither would regard it necessarily as a strategic attack justifying strategic nuclear response. Such discussion might also facilitate the explicit or implicit negotiations leading to recognized limits, which would have to take place after war broke out.

Unilateral discussion of limited war, such as has been going on in the United States, can also serve this goal by making American attitudes towards limited war clear to the Soviet Union, and making clearer the way that America would pursue limits if war did break out. A prewar understanding to keep open a channel of communication, should a limited war break out between the two sides, could help. Also, an understanding might be reached not to initiate the use of certain types of weapons in a limited war; nuclear weapons have received attention.*

In addition, both sides might agree to accept mediation, conciliation, and perhaps arbitration services of neutrals, the U.N. or other groups. In effect, during every limited war, arms control agreements are constantly being made either explicitly or implicitly; each side is agreeing conditionally not to do certain things.

It should be recognized that there may be a cost involved in agreeing to measures which serve to keep local wars limited. Just as agreements that stabilize the strategic balance may make local war more likely, so agreements which serve to facilitate keeping local wars limited may make the outbreak of local war more likely. If one of the things that prevents local wars is the fear of both sides that it will spiral to total war, then agreements which make it less likely that this will happen may end up making local war more likely. On the other hand this could be a reasonable price for greater assurance that local war will not go to total war.

* For a discussion of the possible role of arms control in relation to the use of nuclear weapons in limited war, see Morton H. Halperin, "Nuclear Weapons and Limited War," *The Journal of Conflict Resolution*, forthcoming.

Chapter 3

ARMS CONTROL
AND THE ARMS RACE

In addition to the immediate dangers of general and local war, arms control can be concerned with restraining and tranquilizing the arms race. This chapter discusses the possible functions of arms control in moderating and making less dangerous the current arms race.

MISCHIEF

There are a number of actions short of war that we and our allies and our enemies might jointly wish to abstain from, in the interest of reducing false alarms, accidents that might lead to war, dangerous crises, an excessive accumulation of threats and challenges, or just excessive tension and suspense. Espionage, especially the clumsy kind, may be an example; other forms of intrusion into each other's territory, especially the kind that may seem insulting or arrogant or the kind that may be designed to elicit a military response that the intruder can study, are also of this sort. There are possibilities of interfering with each other's communications, jamming each other's warning systems, "spoofing" each other's warning systems with mock attacks or the deliberate creation of fake accidents (like "inadvertently" dragging up each other's undersea cables) that are evidently mischievous and provocative though they do not qualify as overt hostile acts. There may also be harassments and demonstrations, such as testing weapons near each other's countries or interfering with each other's shipping, that might be attractive by their power to intimidate, to coerce or to create dissension among allies. Finally, there are possibilities of surreptitious military action, "secret military war," that both sides might consciously engage in, such as destroying each other's satellites or chasing each other's submarines.

The characteristic of most of these potentially provocative forms of behavior is that they may from time to time appeal to one side or the other as an advantageous device, but when used by both sides may tend to raise the danger of war without appreciable net advantage to either side. And either side can do these things; or, if it cannot readily do some of them, it can do others. There is furthermore the possibility that if the general level of mischievous and provocative activity gets above some threshold, it may tend to escalate and get out of hand. Many of these actions have the character of a "dare," such that neither side can afford to let them pass but has to respond, perhaps respond in a dominant way that preserves face and gets the upper hand or the last word, with a snowballing effect.

It is noteworthy that we already abstain from quite an array of such actions without formal agreement, without direct communication about it, without even an appreciation that this in itself is a form of arms control — of military cooperation between enemies. But an important reason for our abstaining, or the Soviet's abstaining, from quite a variety of either deliberately provocative actions or unilaterally advantageous actions that would tend to be provocative, must be the appreciation that there is some value in our both abstaining, rather than our both engaging in them, and little likelihood that one side alone can engage in them to an appreciable extent without the other side's joining in. This is, therefore, a very informal kind of arms control. And it is an important one.

It also illustrates that cooperative abstention from potentially dangerous military action is possible, and can be arrived at in quite informal ways. The process is not wholly unlike the rather tacit process of arriving at limits in war; one might call it "limited cold war." The process by which we arrive, or have arrived, at such limitations as we and the Russians presently observe, may well be worth studying, partly to assure that we do not prejudice by neglect such understandings as we already have but also to see whether there are additional opportunities which, if we become conscious of them, can be secured. Studying some of the arms restraints that we already observe is an important means of discovering what kinds of arms limitations are possible, particularly the kinds that are possible in the absence of overt political settlements.

INTELLIGENCE

"Arms race" refers to the interaction between two or more adversaries' military programs, to a tendency for each side's program to respond to what the other is doing. The arms level that each is willing to support depends on the level the other side has reached. This is true whether each side is trying to be far ahead of the other, trying only to keep up with the other, or one is trying to maintain superiority and the other trying to avoid too serious an inferiority.

Each side is guided by its *estimate* of what the other side is doing. If each greatly exaggerates what the other is doing, the competition is exacerbated; if each underestimates the other's accomplishments the race will be damped. But in matters as uncertain as strategic warfare, neither can be certain of its estimate of the other's military potential. In the absence of reliable evidence of what the other is doing, each may feel obliged to err on the "safe" side — to impute an extreme capability and potential to the other. (If each does this, and responds accordingly, the result may actually bear out the extreme estimates!)

The possibility exists, therefore, that the arms race might be damped if each side possessed better information about what the other is doing. Certainly, if it were clear that each participant invariably exaggerated the other's accomplishments, improving the estimates of what each other is doing could reassure them and slow them down. True, if usual behavior were to rationalize a sense of superiority by underestimating the other's program, improved estimates would stimulate weapon programs. And there are some asymmetrical possibilities. But the most important circumstance in which both sides might gain from an improvement in intelligence about each other's military strength is that in which information on both sides (or perhaps just on one side) is so poor, and is recognized to be so poor, that there are strong motivations to err on the upward side. The "missile gap" that one feels obliged to assume to exist in the absence of reliable information, may substantially exceed the actual gap, causing a more frantic increase in armaments than would be undertaken with better information. And it may induce reciprocal action on the other side.

It is interesting that even if intelligence is poor on one side alone, both might have an interest in improving the flow of intelligence. Clearly, our arms program is in response to what we take the Soviet military posture to be. If the Soviets in fact exaggerate our program, and respond with an accelerated program of their own, our own program (as a response to the Soviet program) will tend to be larger than it would otherwise be. Improving Soviet understanding of our military posture in this hypothetical case might relieve them of some of the need for such a large military program of their own; and if in fact their program were curtailed, presumably ours could be (and rationally so) in response. (The example can be turned around, of course.)

This assumes that the character of the arms race is at least potentially stable. If in fact we want to have a force that is substantially greater than the Soviet's, and if they want to have a force substantially superior to ours, with perfect information we will both have insatiable programs. If instead each of us feels reasonably secure as long as the other never achieves, say, a two-to-one superiority in large missiles, and if neither is very confident that it could get far enough ahead to have a dominant superiority, then with perfect information force levels could become stabilized. They could even be reduced if each side felt enough budgetary pressure to be content with, say, 80 per cent of the other's missile strength. This numerical example is artificial but does illustrate the concept of a potentially stable or potentially unstable arms race.

What has been said about military strength might be true also of military research and development; an expensive search for exotic defensive weapons might be undertaken or not according as one believes the other side to be undertaking a frantic and expensive search for exotic offensive weapons. The same principle might apply to civil defense; there is some possibility that support in this country for a civil defense program would be stimulated by reliable information of a large, sensibly designed, Soviet civil defense program.

The principle may also apply to limited war. If we and the Soviets are in fact prepared to abstain, say, from the use of nuclear weapons in a particular limited war, reliable intelligence indicating this fact might make it more likely that the limitations could be adhered to. If, for example, we have a high-explosive limited war capability and the Soviets do not know it, they may assume that from the outset we will use nuclear weapons; this could induce them to use nuclears at the outset; knowing that they fail to appreciate our high-explosive capability may force us to anticipate their use of nuclears and to introduce nuclears at the outset ourselves.

It is possible, therefore, that an exchange of inspection facilities could improve each side's intelligence about the other's programs in ways that stabilize and dampen the arms race. It could be argued, though, that either could do this unilaterally without any cooperative arrangements. There are, however, problems in doing it unilaterally. A main one is the difficulty of providing an enemy with information that would stabilize the arms race without at the same time giving information that runs counter to other objectives discussed above. If the Russians think that by letting us count their missiles and launching sites we get the targeting information we may need for an attack, they will not be interested. For reasons like this it may take some cooperative arrangements, formal or informal, to provide the intelligence that might be stabilizing with safeguards to preclude other intelligence from leaking through that would be destabilizing.

Intelligence arrangements — both those that yield good intelligence and those that work faultily — can do harm as well as good, and some aspects of the arms race may be enhanced, rather than damped, by better information, but this is not necessarily a bad thing. If better intelligence discloses that our retaliatory forces are more vulnerable than we thought, we may take steps that would look superficially like an aggravated arms race but that in fact would reduce incentives towards initiation of war.

It deserves to be emphasized — especially to the Soviets — that *secrecy* may be a dangerous and unreliable support for strategic security. Missile and air forces that depend for their protection on universal secrecy — on secrecy of their fixed location — are vulnerable to improved intelligence. And it may be in the nature of an intelligence break-through that the loss of secrecy is sudden and extensive. (The problem may not be one of finding a large number of independent sites, one after another, but of knowing what to look for or how to interpret intelligence already available; when the key is discovered, it may decipher a great deal.) Furthermore, the strategic force that depends on such secrecy can never be confident of its secret. If secrecy appears a cheap and attractive way of gaining security for the strategic forces — cheaper than mobility, dispersal, hardening, diversification, and warning systems — it is also a risky one. If arms control is inconsistent with such secrecy, or impairs it, the response should not be to rely less on arms control but to rely less on secrecy. The development by the Soviets of strategic forces that depend less on universal secrecy may be a proper subject of arms negotiations.

TECHNOLOGY

The current "arms race" might be termed a *qualitative* one. It mainly involves the development of new weapons and new delivery systems, rather than the accumulation of larger quantities of existing weapons. Although it has been argued that qualitative races have been historically more stable than quantitative ones, the present race seems unstable because of the uncertainty in technology and the danger of a decisive break-through. Uncertainty means that each side must be prepared to spend a great deal of money; it also means a constant fear on either side that the other has developed a dominant position, or will do so, or will fear the first to do so, with the resulting danger of premeditated or pre-emptive attack.

In addition is the possibility of break-throughs which, though available to both sides, would be seriously destabilizing. An example that tends in this direction is the improvement in missile accuracy that has already occurred, relative to what was expected a few years ago. Developments of this sort increase the likelihood that an attack on retaliatory forces would succeed, and thus increase the dangers of premeditated and pre-emptive attack.

Measures to slow down or to stabilize the technological race might be approached cooperatively at a number of different points. These would include the research stage, the development stage, the testing stage, and the stage of updating and improving weapons. One can envision agreements to forego testing, for example in connection with improved guidance of missiles. Or one can envision an agreement that permitted development and testing of new guidance, but not the placing of new guidance systems in missiles. There are problems with each of these. Limitations on research are difficult to enforce because it is never really clear what sort of research is going to lead to useful military techniques. There is also the problem of preventing military development while permitting peaceful development. It is, for example, probably feasible, but by no means easy, to devise control mechanisms and agreements that would retard the development of military missiles while permitting some development and use of outer-space vehicles.

Over the next few years technological developments may be stabilizing rather than destabilizing. Missile systems will likely be produced that are less vulnerable than present weapons. Such forces could reduce greatly the danger of both premeditated and pre-emptive attack. On the other hand, break-throughs might occur that would be highly destabilizing.

THE SPREAD OF WEAPONS

A major function of arms control may be to prevent the giving (selling) of weapons to other countries, and to prevent the spread of the technology for producing weapons. The "Nth" country problem has given a major impetus to the drive for nuclear-weapons control. Many feel that only through some international agreement can the spread of nuclear weapons to other countries be prevented.*

Such an agreement might be to the advantage of both the United States and the Soviet Union. It might be valuable in strengthening Soviet resistance to Chinese demands for nuclear weapons. Much of the interest in the nuclear-test suspension has come to center on the possible effect of slowing down, or stopping, the production or acquisition of such weapons by countries that do not now produce them.

This function of arms control applies to other weapons as well as nuclears. Regional arms embargoes, for Africa or the Middle East, have been suggested. The spread of nuclear weapons and missiles to other countries might increase the danger of accidental war, or "catalytic war." It would also facilitate nuclear threats by irresponsible governments. Arms embargoes may also inhibit local wars that are not only themselves deplorable but threaten to draw in major powers and major weapons.

* For a discussion of the capabilities needed to produce nuclear weapons and the resources of various "Nth" countries, see The National Planning Association, *The Nth Country Problem and Arms Control* (Washington: National Planning Association, 1960).

It seems very likely that the world would be more dangerous if a dozen or so countries developed nuclear capabilities. One of the clearest ways that arms control may benefit both sides in the East-West antagonism is to prevent the spread of these weapons and this technology.*

* For an excellent statement of the contrary case — that the spread of nuclear weapons is not necessarily deplorable and that the time may not be ripe to deal with the "Nth" country problem — see Fred C. Iklé, "Nth Countries and Disarmament," *Bulletin of the Atomic Scientists* XVI (December 1960) 383–90.

PART II

THE EVALUATION OF ARMS-CONTROL PROPOSALS

Chapter 4

POLITICAL—MILITARY
INTERRELATIONS

The evaluation of any arms proposal will depend
on its specific contents; nevertheless, it is possible to lay out some
general guides. Our attention will be mainly on military evaluation; we shall deal only briefly with the more general political implications.

The evaluation of any arms agreement must consider three broad
possibilities: that the agreement will operate as planned; that one
or both sides will cheat and get away with it; that at some point in
time the agreement will break down and both sides will resume,
openly, the prohibited activities, withdraw the concessions, and
cease to cooperate. Each of these contingencies poses different
problems of evaluation.

An arms agreement is not necessarily advantageous either from
a military or political point of view just because it operates as intended. Much of the dispute over the test ban, for example, has
concerned whether the Russians could or would cheat. But the first
question to be asked is: If the Russians *do not* cheat, what will be
the effect of the test ban on the military environment? Is it to the
advantage of the United States to negotiate a test ban even if both
sides live up to it?

Of course one must evaluate the possibilities of cheating, as well.
What is the *likelihood* of cheating? What are the consequences of
cheating? What does one side or the other gain, if it cheats and
gets away with it? What do both sides get if both cheat? These
questions depend, in turn, on the likelihood that cheating will be

43

discovered, and on what the recourse is in that event. Cheating, of course, may be of various kinds and degrees.

One has to consider the possibility that the agreement will break down, either because one or both sides entered the agreement with the idea that at some future date they could gain a military or political advantage by renouncing the agreement, or because at some point in time one or both sides suddenly find the agreement intolerable. The breakdown may come at a moment of acute political crisis; it may come because of a change of regime in one country. It may come during the early stages of the agreement when both sides are moving towards the agreed posture, or at a later stage when they have gotten into the posture envisaged in the agreement. It is important to ask how likely it is that one side will break the agreement, and what it gains by participating for a time and then beginning the race anew.

For each of these three possibilities — that the agreement works, that it is cheated on, that it breaks down — there are military and political implications. No agreement can buy everything. An agreement may have political costs and military gains. An agreement may contribute to some functions discussed in Part I and detract from others. It is only in relation to a *particular* agreement that one can arrive at a balance of political and military costs and benefits.*

East-West Relations

One must ask: Will the agreement contribute to the possibility of a genuine *détente* between East and West? Will it help to establish a system of world law and a process of peaceful change? What effect will the agreement have on relations between the United States and the Soviet Union? An arms agreement that leads to cooperation may produce a feeling that the two sides have more in common than they have apart. It may create an awareness of the possibility of cooperation between East and West, and pave the way for future arms agreements and cooperation in dealing with such problems as the growing power of China.

On the other hand, the contact between the United States and

* For an extended evaluation of the nuclear-test ban using the framework presented here see Donald G. Brennan and Morton H. Halperin, "Policy Considerations of a Nuclear Test Ban," to appear in Brennan (ed.) *Arms Control, Disarmament, and National Security.*

the Soviet Union made necessary by an arms agreement may affect relations adversely. Continuous inspection might produce continuous irritation. Each side might suspect the other's inspection to be espionage. Each might feel that the other was demanding to see what it had no right to see, or that its own inspectors were being denied the right to see what they had to see to monitor the agreement effectively. Arms control might worsen tensions rather than relieve them.

A second effect that arms control might have on East-West relations is in the ways that it serves to alter American and Soviet conduct. If an agreement is successful and both sides feel that it contributes to their security, it may inhibit military and political activities that would put the agreement in jeopardy. A nuclear-test ban that inhibited the spread of nuclear weapons to America's European allies could be put in jeopardy by a Soviet attempt at nuclear blackmail against West European countries. Thus if a test ban had gone into effect and the Soviets had derived major benefits from it, they might refrain from conduct that would destroy the agreement.

China

China poses special difficulties for political and military evaluation of any arms agreement. The Chinese may be especially irritated by inspection; the Chinese may be unwilling to sign and less interested in preserving an agreement if it interferes with their goals in Asia. The political evaluation of an agreement that needs to include China must take the legal and diplomatic consequences into account; an agreement that included China would raise the issue of China's entrance into the United Nations and diplomatic recognition by the United States. Here one has to weigh the possible gains, in terms of modifying and moderating Chinese policy, against the costs of giving China greater influence in world affairs and a greater voice in future arms control and diplomatic negotiations. If China were left out of an agreement, special problems would arise. For some forms of arms control (e.g., nuclear-test ban) one has to consider the possibility of Soviet violation by arrangements with the Chinese. If an agreement excludes China one has to consider that the Chinese may be able to disrupt the agreement when they wish to, by creating a crisis that forces the West into violation of the agreement to protect its security interests. In evaluating any arms control, the strategic position of the Chinese and the political costs and gains of including them will thus often be central issues.

Other Countries

Neutralist opinion is also important. As the 1960 General Assembly session again made clear, the neutral nations can exert pressure on the East and the West in relation to arms agreements. Many neutralist nations seem to favor disarmament both because they fear war and because they expect that significant sums of money will be made available for their development after major East-West disarmament occurs.

Closely related is the so-called Nth-country problem: the spread of nuclear weapons and ballistic missiles to fourth, fifth, and other powers. Although there are losses involved in seeking to halt the spread of nuclear weapons, it may well be to the interests of both the United States and the Soviet Union to do so. The problem is that many of the countries that are likely to get nuclear weapons in the next several years are allies of the United States. This brings into focus, sharply, the effect of arms control on America's allies. Many American allies and, particularly, many opposition groups within allied countries are eager for agreements that would reduce tensions. There will be pressure in many instances from allied countries (as there has been from Great Britain on the test ban) to modify positions in order to reach agreement with the Soviet Union.

On the other hand, many types of arms agreements are likely to produce negative results in terms of America's relations with her allies. Direct Soviet-American negotiations may be necessary, and are usually looked upon with suspicion by the other members of NATO. An agreement not to share nuclear weapons with third countries may be felt undesirable by some of the NATO states. Any agreement that tends to neutralize American strategic forces vis-à-vis Soviet forces might alarm countries that depend on American strategic power to deter a Soviet attack on them. The United States might have to increase its direct military support if it were to agree to arms control that lessened the value of its strategic forces for the defense of local areas. Certain arms agreements might be interpreted as undermining the alliance and the ability of the senior partner to protect the others.

Further Arms Control

Agreements are likely to have long-range political consequences as well as more immediate effects. These merge in the possibility that an arms agreement will lead to further arms negotiations and agreements between the two sides. In evaluating any particular proposal, it has to be considered whether, if this agreement fails, future arms control will be impossible or unlikely. *Successful* working of a particular agreement can increase the likelihood of further, more far-reaching, arms control; poor agreements may discredit and retard arms regulation.

A particular arms agreement may be desired because it paves the way for further arms control. A limited agreement may help to test the efficiency of various inspection techniques and to discover ways of improving them. It may help to discover what efforts both sides are willing to make to convince each other that they are not cheating. It may help to try international control machinery, to discover kinks in recruiting or communications, or to test how a voting mechanism works and whether the international machinery can accomplish what it is supposed to accomplish.

Each country may, furthermore, want to check the effect of any agreement on its internal administration and morale, particularly in its military services. Legal problems may be more easily handled initially for a limited agreement. A limited agreement might be valuable for discovering public attitudes towards inspectorates, and how they are affected by the role the inspectorate performs. Finally, each side may want to gauge the effect any agreement has on the international political environment, and on its ability to pursue its goals by other methods. In these various ways, limited measures of arms control may be useful preliminaries to more ambitious arrangements.

It may also be the case that some first steps at arms control would alter the political climate, externally or internally, in a way that would make possible (or impossible) more comprehensive schemes. In any event, whatever the initial motives and occurrences that bring particular measures of arms control into prominence, the measures may acquire a symbolic value, as a "test case," and become at least as important for their implications for subsequent negotiations as for their intrinsic merits. This seems to have been true of the nuclear-test discussions.

Domestic Politics

There are also domestic political effects of an agreement. The party in power may have to consider the effect on its electoral successes of negotiating seriously, of arriving at an agreement, and of putting into effect arms agreements that involve large-scale military changes, budgetary changes, or inspection within the country. While the successful negotiation of a nuclear-test treaty will not make it less imperative for the United States to develop invulnerable strategic forces and large-scale conventional forces, it might be that the electorate and even some policy makers within the United States would take the nuclear-test agreement as a symbol of a new international situation which no longer made it necessary to have even the present level of military forces.

We have discussed international and domestic political factors only in broad outline. While we shall give more space in this book to the military evaluation of arms proposals, we again emphasize that this disproportion reflects the orientation we have brought to the present study, not an insistence that military factors ought to dominate the others. We emphasize that the political *and* military factors must be considered, and that the balancing can be done only in terms of a *particular* agreement.

Chapter 5

THE STRATEGIC
BALANCE

W<small>HAT</small> kinds of arms arrangements would, and
what kinds would not, increase the security of the participants and
the rest of the world against the dangers of war and aggression?
Much current discussion suggests that there are but two principal
desiderata. The first is that the *general level of armaments*, some-
how measured, be reduced; the second is that the *ratio* of strengths
of the two blocs (or relative strengths of the main participants) not
become too disaligned, that an appropriate "balance" be maintained in the reduction. Both considerations are implied in such
phrases as "balanced reduction," "phased reduction," or "proportionate reduction" of armaments. It is of course recognized that a
distinction has to be made between strategic and tactical forces,
nuclear and conventional forces, missiles and manpower, and so
forth; but even in this connection, the problem seems to be widely
viewed as one of maintaining an appropriate balance between adversaries, and something like proportionate reductions across the
board is often referred to as a crude but satisfactory way around
this complication.

The discussion in Part I should have made clear that the strategic
evaluation of an arms-control proposal, particularly of a comprehensive proposal, involves a complex of considerations that are not
easily summarized in the simple notion of a "balanced reduction"
of military forces. While it seems almost certain that any comprehensive and explicit arms accommodation between the two main
power blocs would, as a practical matter, entail a reduction in mili-

49

tary forces and that the relative strengths of the two blocs will be a major consideration, it is not at all certain — in fact, it is unlikely — that these two considerations should be dominant. There are many others: the vulnerability of strategic weapons to attack; the susceptibility of weapon systems to accident or false alarm; the reliability of command and communication arrangements; the susceptibility of weapon systems to sudden technological obsolescence; the confidence with which each side can estimate the capabilities of the opponent's weapons; the reaction time that weapon systems allow to decision-makers in a crisis; the susceptibility of weapon systems to control and restraint in the event of war; the suitability of weapon systems for blackmail, intimidation, wars of nerves, and general mischief; and the effects of different weapon systems on the internal relations within alliances. These are important considerations and are not closely enough correlated with the general *level* of weapons on both sides or the simple arithmetical *ratio* of strength between the power blocs to permit "balanced reduction of forces" to be an adequate description of the strategic objective of arms control.

Stability

The concept of "stability" is often adduced as a third consideration. It is useful, though still incomplete. A "balance of deterrence" — a situation in which the incentives on both sides to initiate war are outweighed by the disincentives — is described as "stable" when it is reasonably secure against shocks, alarms and perturbations. That is, it is "stable" when political events, internal or external to the countries involved, technological change, accidents, false alarms, misunderstandings, crises, limited wars, or changes in the intelligence available to both sides, are unlikely to disturb the incentives sufficiently to make mutual deterrence fail. This concept of "stability" is a fuzzy one, partly because there is no clear-cut agreement among those who use the term on precisely what the trends and events are that might upset the balance and what the relative likelihoods are. The concept is also inadequate to cover all the considerations left out of the two usual ones (*level* and *ratio*) mentioned above; it could not, for example, be extended to cover the scale of unintended damage in the event of war, without its becoming just a synonym for everything important and desirable in the field of arms control. It does, nevertheless, cover a set of important considerations ranging from the vulnerability of retaliatory weapons themselves to the security of command and control arrangements, dependence on fallible warning systems, the urgency of decisions based on incomplete information, and the potential for misunderstanding that may be involved in the mode of deployment of weapons.

Qualitative and Quantitative Limitations

To some extent a distinction can be made between the quantitative and the qualitative aspects of arms control. In earlier eras there was interest in the limitation of offensive weapons in contrast to defensive weapons, of weapons that were unnecessarily cruel, or of weapons that involved civil damage all out of proportion to their military accomplishments. The present era is one in which important distinctions can be made; but the terms "offensive" and "defensive" are misleading, and the concept of "retaliation" is largely punitive rather than military. The distinction between a "first-strike" and a "second-strike" military capability, however, is a crude but useful distinction.

The distinction is crude because almost any weapon capable of firing back in retaliation is worth something in a first strike, or can be adapted to the purpose. And almost any weapon capable of launching an attack aimed at disarming the enemy would have some prospect of delivering retaliatory damage in the event it were attacked first. One can kill a rabbit with an elephant gun, and can probably kill an elephant with .22 rifles if enough of them are skillfully used; but there is a distinction between a rabbit gun and an elephant gun, and there is a distinction, though unfortunately not as striking, between the modern strategic weapons particularly suitable for a disarming attack on the enemy, and those that are particularly suitable for threatening retaliation if attacked first. On the whole, it costs money to make a retaliatory system reasonably secure against attack; for a given outlay, one gets less of a first-strike capability as a by-product of procuring a second-strike capability than if one ignores the second-strike qualities and invests the available military resources in a maximum first-strike capability. This distinction refers, it must be emphasized, to the entire weapon system, not just to the missiles or the aircraft: to the base configuration, the hardening or the mobility, the communications, the warning system, and everything else that goes to make up the strategic force. It furthermore is a distinction that is not absolute, but relative to the enemy's own forces: a missile-carrying submarine may be a useful first-strike weapon if the enemy has fixed land-based missiles near his shores, but not if he, too, has his missiles under water.

The distinction should not be pressed too far. A "second-strike" capability is not necessarily just a punitive retaliatory capability; it might include provision for attacking such enemy weapons as had not yet been launched. It might also include active and passive defense of the homeland, of the kind that would be involved (and would be more effective) in a first-strike force. Similarly, a first-strike force would not necessarily be one that depended solely or even mainly on surprise; certainly, a first-strike force that is used to threaten a major war in a hope of achieving objectives without a war must be one that, if war comes, enjoys some security against a pre-emptive blow. Furthermore, to the extent that a general or strategic war could be limited in its scope or intent instead of being an indiscriminately "all-out" affair, the distinction between first strike and second strike is blurred. These qualifications are important, but do not wholly detract from the usefulness of the distinction.

Offensive and Defensive Weapons

It is important to note that the old distinctions between offensive and defensive weapons are quite inapplicable in the present era, and are more nearly applicable in reverse. Weapons that are particularly effective against enemy weapons, and capable of launching a "disarming" attack, are precisely the weapons needed for the initiation of war. Weapons that are potent against populations, urban complexes, and economic assets have essentially a punitive rather than military quality. They are capable of retaliating, and of threatening retaliation, but are incapable of disarming the enemy and thus give their possessor little incentive or none at all to launch an attack. In that sense they may be reassuring to the other side.

In this connection, there are some logical similarities between weapons designed to destroy enemy forces before they are launched and active defenses designed to destroy them as they approach one's own country. To launch a major attack with some assurance against insupportable retaliation, one needs reasonable prospects either of destroying enemy weapons before they are committed, or of destroying them in flight, or of evading their effects by mobility, sheltering, or evacuation. In that sense, *defensive* measures may be at least as characteristic of a first-strike strategic force as of a purely retaliatory force. They do, of course, differ from the so-called "counter-force" weapons (those that seek to destroy enemy weapons before they are committed) in that defensive weapons themselves have usually tended to be the type that can only respond to an enemy initiative and not take initiative themselves.

It is worth observing in this connection that even passive defenses of the population, like fallout shelters and evacuation procedures, food stockpiles or organizational arrangements for the aftermath of war, are as natural a component of a first-strike force as they are a supplement to a purely retaliatory force. While this observation cannot do justice to the complex and important question of civil defense, it does help to illustrate that the traditional distinction among weapon systems, the traditional qualitative arms-control categories, are misleading in the present era of deterrence.

The missile-carrying submarine is an important illustration of the complexities involved. In some discussions this weapon system has been viewed as a deplorable extension of the arms race into a new medium. The fact that an enemy submarine can be close to one's own borders unobserved is especially disturbing; and the difficulties of anti-submarine warfare are viewed with alarm. But there is a growing recognition that the Polaris submarine may embody many of the qualities that we and our potential enemies would be seeking through arms control to embody in our strategic-weapon systems. If in fact the submarine proves to be reasonably invulnerable, capable of deliberate response, able to maintain communications, and not susceptible to accidents of a provocative sort nor prone to create false alarm, it may prove to be an ideally "retaliatory" and "deterrent" weapon, particularly if possessed by both sides (or if the side that does not possess them enjoys some equivalent invulnerability). It is probably also true, roughly speaking, that the submarine achieves these qualities at some expense: either side may be able to afford this kind of weapon system better if the other's weapons are not so threatening as to stimulate a strong desire for a pre-emptive capability.

Asymmetries in the Limitations

The Polaris system also reminds us that a comprehensive arms-control program may involve important asymmetries, or striking differences between the weapon systems allowed to the two power blocs. There is no reason to believe that we and the Soviets would be equally interested in this particular weapon system. For reasons that range from geography to military tradition, from intelligence and secrecy to technology, from the nature of our alliances to the character of our space program, the Western alliance and the Soviet bloc may develop very different interests in, or attitudes towards, the submarine as a strategic weapon. An implication of this is that any comprehensive arms-control program might have to recognize that the basic strategic weapons on both sides would be quite dissimilar. This in turn would make it difficult to arrive at any simple, durable, and reasonable comparison between the weapons on both sides; a submarine with 16 missiles of a certain accuracy and reliability, carrying a certain nuclear warhead, on station a certain fraction of time, with a certain reaction time depending on its communications and its distance from an ideal launching point, admits of no simple obvious comparison with, say, a base complex of hard or soft, large, land-based missiles, or a railroad train with a certain number of smaller missiles spending a certain fraction of its time in a state of readiness, with a certain vulnerability to detection and destruction. This is emphasized not because it makes arms control more difficult (which it probably does, but not strikingly so) but because it reminds us that certain asymmetries under arms control are inevitable.

Diversification of Weapons

While the qualities of particular weapon systems deserve careful attention, it is important not to push too far the search for the "ideal" weapon, under arms control as under the uncontrolled arms race. An important reason is that diversification itself may be strategically important, and even more so in a partially disarmed world. If we want strategic military forces on both sides that lend "stability" to the balance of deterrence — weapons that are unlikely to be substantially destroyed in an enemy attack, weapons that are unlikely to become suddenly impotent because of a technological revolution — there are powerful reasons for believing that a diversified retaliatory system is better than one built around a single weapon or a single operating concept. To restate this in a way that makes its arms-control implications clear: If the participants in a comprehensive arms-control arrangement want security, simultaneous with a reduction in the level of armaments, a diversified mix of retaliatory weapons may permit a lower level of *total* armaments than would be acceptable if each has to rely on a single weapon system.

The reasons why this is so are many. One is that the different weapon systems may pose sufficiently different kinds of targets as to complicate the coordination problem. Synchronizing a no-warning strike may be harder when the targets are in different places, with different characteristics, different environments, etc. Second, by requiring a diversity of attack, they may increase the ways that the defender can get intelligence. Third, if one exploits this possibility of diversity, he may design his weapon system, particularly with respect to its size and scope, in order to optimize the cost advantage involved — to maximize the enemy's costs in being able to deal with all the defender's weapon systems simultaneously. Fourth, by moving into new systems and environments one may force the attacker to prepare his attacking weapons subject to serious uncertainty about the target they will have to be used on. Fifth, it increases the amount and kinds of intelligence the attacker needs. And sixth — a point that deserves to be emphasized — it must reduce greatly the confidence of any political decision-maker in the estimates that his experts give him about the outcome of a war.

It is important to stress that the diversified weapon system might well be more expensive than one that concentrates on the single "best" system. There are overhead costs in the development, production, and operation of strategic weapons; greater variety would entail smaller scale exploitation of each weapon system. This may be a price worth paying, and is emphasized here as a further reminder that, while fewer weapons may be cheaper than more weapons, "better" weapons may not be cheaper than "worse" ones.

Stability and Size of Forces

The foregoing discussion has treated the qualitative issues separately from the quantitative. It has suggested that the "stability" and other important characteristics of weapons are separate from the question of numbers or size. There is a connection, however, between the qualitative and the quantitative characteristics. The stability of the weapon systems on both sides may itself be a function of the numbers of weapons and the numbers of targets they present to each other. Whether a strategic force is, and appears to be, essentially designed to carry out a threat of retaliation, and hence suitable for deterrence, or instead is designed for maximum success in a sudden attack on the enemy, to some extent depends on the very size of the force itself.

This is obvious when one side tries, or each tries, to achieve such numerical dominance that it could virtually preclude retaliation by an overwhelming attack. But the point to be emphasized here is that even if some rough equality is achieved and maintained in the balance of forces between the two sides, through arms control or otherwise, the *level* of forces on both sides may be an important determinant of the stability of that balance.

The reason is that the outcome of a general war, as perceived by either side, is not simply a function of the ratio of forces. That ratio may determine, very crudely speaking, what *fraction* of the victim's forces are capable of retaliating if one side launches a sudden attack on the other; but that fraction would be large or small in absolute size, and will imply larger or smaller retaliatory destruction, depending on the absolute level at the outset.

To illustrate the point, consider a situation in which one side has, say, half again as many weapons as the other. Suppose that — taking into account how the strategic forces are clustered in their bases and what kinds of target they offer to each other, and taking into account the accuracy of the weapons, target-location, and intelligence — every weapon fired in a well-coordinated surprise attack has about a 75 per cent chance of destroying an enemy weapon. Two weapons fired at the same target would have a fifteen-sixteenths chance of destroying the target. Then 150 weapons fired at 100 weapons would be expected to destroy about 84 weapons on the other side, leaving about 16 with which the victim could attempt retaliation in the hostile and disorganized environment in which he then found himself. Fifteen hundred weapons fired at 1,000 could, crudely speaking, then be expected to destroy a similar proportion, say, about 840, leaving about 160 with which the victim could attempt retaliation. The ratio of weapons in both cases is the same; the retaliatory damage to be anticipated by the attacker, however, may be strikingly different, since he faces a residual force of 16 or 160 depending on the initial scale of military forces on both sides.

This crude illustration is hardly a model of modern warfare, and ignores especially the interdependencies among weapons that rely on the same communications, warning, and so forth. Nevertheless it illustrates a valid and important point: that the *level* of forces on both sides, not simply the *ratio*, is an important determinant of the prospective scale of retaliation, and of the potency of deterrence.

This is hardly an argument for encouraging a maximum of weapons on both sides. (The point elaborated here has dealt only with the *deterrent* qualities of the strategic forces; there are also the questions, mentioned in Part I, of whether larger forces are conducive to keeping limited a war once it starts, and whether larger forces might be more susceptible to "accidents" of some sort. Neither of these questions admits of a simple answer.) It is an argument, however, that must be weighed in the balance with other considerations in deciding how low a level of forces on both sides might be contemplated in an arms-control arrangement that wished to preserve and stabilize the deterrent balance.

It is essentially this consideration and the fact that very small forces are more vulnerable to a clandestine attacking force that lead many who concern themselves with arms control to think of a goal well short of the complete elimination of strategic weapons. It is not simply that a reduction to modest levels is a less ambitious goal. It is that the situation may become safer in the event of war, and more stable with respect to the likelihood of war, if forces are substantially reduced, but that *beyond a certain point* further reduction may increase both the fears and the temptations that aggravate the likelihood of war.

This is not said to settle the question of whether total disarmament with respect to strategic weapons is the wrong goal. The point is rather that, beyond a certain point in the reduction of retaliatory weapons on both sides, one must recognize that the balance of deterrence is being dismantled in exchange for the advantages of total disarmament. One has to consider whether the exchange is a profitable one, and to recognize that the rationale for proceeding towards zero must be different from the original rationale for reducing to moderate levels. One may also have to recognize that, no matter how nicely the balance *between* the opposing forces may be kept — no matter how well some *ratio* of forces is preserved in the process of arms reduction — the greater security sought at some extremely low level of forces may require passing through a region of greater insecurity, a region where forces are too small for mutual deterrence and too large for the hoped-for benefits of a totally (or nearly) disarmed world to compensate for the disappearance of mutual deterrence.

Stability vs. Disarmament

The concept of "stabilized deterrence" has recently come into vogue as a characterization of a particular school of arms control. Those who wish to reduce armaments and those who wish to stabilize deterrence are contrasted. Up to a point the contrast is useful, and identifies a difference in emphasis. But the two objectives are not alternatives. Whatever the level of armaments, more stability is better than less. Even with zero armaments, there is still a problem of deterring rearmament; and the stability of this deterrence may depend on much the same considerations that stabilized nuclear deterrence depends on in an armed world — namely, the elimination of the advantage in going first, in starting rearmament as in starting a war; increasing the tolerance of the system to errors in judgment or mistaken intentions; minimizing the haste with which decisions to initiate rearmament or to initiate war must be taken; structuring the incentives so that, whatever the capabilities, the mutually destructive or risky action is not initiated.

"Stabilized deterrence" is also sometimes equated with stabilizing the balance of terror. But the greater the stability, the less terror there is. The fear is a function of the instability, of the lack of confidence in the incentives that exist, of anxiety about the need to react with violence to every alarm and threat. Efforts to stabilize deterrence are efforts to tranquilize anxieties and decisions, to strengthen the incentives towards deliberate rather than hasty action, to minimize the alarms and mistakes. To make the initiation of war manifestly profitless, and to provide each side sufficient control over its own decisions to eliminate the inadvertent initiation of war, may substantially deflate the fearsomeness of the balance.

One abstains from crossing the street in the face of onrushing traffic not out of "fear" but simply because one knows better; he takes for granted that the consequences would be disastrous, but he knows that he can control his own actions. Successfully stabilized deterrence, to the extent that it could be achieved, might better be described as an effort to replace the balance of fear with a "balance of prudence."

The search for stability has also been criticized, and can justly be criticized, for expecting too much. We live in a world of technological as well as political uncertainties; the stabilized deterrence of tomorrow may become less stable the day after that. This is a splendid caution about what to expect, and a reminder that to stabilize deterrence is not equivalent to guaranteeing freedom from war. This is no objection to pursuing stabilization vigorously and persistently; we can never be guaranteed against household accidents, but that does not make a safety program futile.

There is an incompatibility, of course, between the notion that war is prevented by some kind of deterrence, and that war is prevented by the eradication of military establishments, military tradition, and military thinking. Stabilizing deterrence is not therefore compatible with all motives for disarmament. On the other hand, some proposals for stabilizing deterrence do involve substantial reduction of force levels; and stabilized deterrence as a concept is not committed in advance to any particular level of destructive power.

The relation between stabilized deterrence and reduced force levels can be indirect as well as direct. One may hope directly to reduce force levels in the interest of minimizing the possible violence in the case of war. One may propose reducing force levels in the interest of stabilizing deterrence. Or one may propose vigorous measures to help stabilize deterrence, in the expectation that force levels will naturally and unilaterally be reduced as a result. Certainly a powerful motivation towards the indefinite build-up of destructive power is a preoccupation with the need to pre-empt the enemy's attack; another is the fear that one's own forces might be so destroyed in the surprise attack that deterrence itself requires an enormous margin for safety. If forces on both sides become fairly invulnerable to pre-emptive attack, the incentive towards larger and larger numbers might be greatly deflated. Reductions in force levels might be reciprocated, in something of a downward spiral. The more the arms race can be diverted into those kinds of qualitative improvements in military force that reduce the danger of war, the less the incentive may be to maintain exorbitant levels of destructive power. Furthermore, the likelihood that all existing explosive potential would be used exhaustively and indiscriminately in the event of war becomes less and less, the more each side designs its military forces for deliberate rather than for hasty actions, the better the control that it maintains over them, and the less obvious advantage there is in attempts to saturate the enemy's country in the hope of nullifying his retaliatory forces.

Stability and Total Disarmament

It is often said or implied that many problems that remain with us under arms control, or that arms control itself may usher in, are due solely to the incompleteness of the disarmament. In a wholly disarmed world, it is asserted, especially one subject to an organized international disciplinary force, the blackmailing threats would be hollow, limited war would be physically unavailable, and even the power to reverse the trend of history and rearm would have been put beyond the reach of national decision.

The argument is quite unpersuasive. In the absence of some effective policing force, primitive war is still possible, rearmament is possible, and primitive wars that last long enough may convert themselves by rapid mobilization into very modern warfare. Nor is primitive warfare necessarily a very attractive alternative to the more modern type, unless the sides are so well-balanced and the supply lines so critical that the tactical defense automatically assumes dominance over the offense.

The "police force" itself poses some genuine problems. Will it rely on "containment" and limited war; or will it rely on the threat of retaliation to keep nations not only confined within their own borders but deprived of weapons and their productive facilities? How will it cope with "creeping rearmament" or with national rearmament that is motivated by the fear that others already are, or soon will be, rearming? Will nations be coerced by other nations' threats of rearmament; and will the international force's deterrent threat (to intervene forcibly, or to retaliate from a distance) against a rearming nation be considered adequate protection? Would it permit defensive alliances among states that are too small to resist alone even technologically primitive aggression by large powers; if so, what rules of "balance of power" will it permit or encourage in respect of military alliances? If a decisive and effective monopoly of military force is brought into existence, one that can act quickly and decisively and against the will of its opponents and the vacillation of its well-wishers, can it be prevented from acting as either a benevolent or a tyrannical despot? And how does it distinguish between external warfare and civil war?

These are not secondary problems to be solved after total disarmament is agreed on, nor are they problems whose solution is held up at the present time only because we lack the will and the political environment to make disarmament possible. These questions are as fundamental as the political and strategic military problems that characterize the present world. They may be easier to manage in an environment of "total disarmament" (including a world with a unified monopoly of military force) than they are in the present world. But they will not be absent.

In this respect, "total disarmament" may not differ as much in character from "arms control" as is sometimes implied. In any of these contingencies, conflict of interest will occur, potential force will always be at hand, and the military technology of the present era and new technology still to come will not have been erased from the records and men's memories.

Chapter 6

LIMITED WAR
AND COLD WAR

ARMS control relates directly and indirectly to local war. Directly, it may affect the forces and weapons available for local war, their geographical deployment, the bases they can operate from, and all the limits and inhibitions that go to make local war limited. Of special importance would be measures controlling or inhibiting the use of nuclear weapons.

Indirectly, arms control may interrelate with local war in a number of ways. To the extent that it reassures the major powers against the outbreak of general war, it may take some of the *risk* out of local war itself. Certainly a main inhibition on the initiation of small war at the present time (as well as an inhibition of enlargements of local war or the introduction of new weapons into them) is the fear of an accident or a spiraling process that may lead to general war. But if the urge to pre-empt is sufficiently calmed down, if false alarms or the responses to them are made less of a danger, if the scale of destruction even in the event of a general war is made to appear less cataclysmic than it otherwise might, one paradoxical result may be to "make the world safe for local war." And if both sides have collaborated in programs to make their own and each others' strategic weapons reasonably indestructible under attack, neither can very credibly threaten deliberate initiation of general war except for the most mortal contingencies.

An implication of this is that local-war arms budgets might substantially increase as a consequence of measures to make general war less likely. In fact, this is a very real possibility in the light of present budgetary controversies. It has been argued in the past that the deterrent threat of general war makes it unnecessary to go to the expense of possessing local-war forces; it has also been argued that nuclear weapons could economize in the forces we need for local war. Some of the present clamor for increasing our expenditure on local-war forces, and especially for conventionally-armed forces, is a direct response to a belief that the balance of deterrence has already made the threat of massive retaliation insufficiently credible to be effective, and a response to a belief that strong inhibitions either do exist or should exist on the introduction of nuclear weapons into local war.

But the influence of arms control on local war is complex. It can be supposed that any substantial measure of arms control would result only from some greater recognition than presently exists of the common interests that we share with our main potential enemies in the avoidance of war and the tranquilization of international violence. To assume comprehensive arms control, or even to assume important limited measures of arms control, and to suppose that in every other respect the world is unchanged from what it might have been, is unreasonable. Thus, the sheer improved understanding on both sides of the need for restraint in our military actions, and the improved ability of both sides to act on that understanding, is probably a prerequisite for any extensive arms control, and would itself undoubtedly entail important ramifications extending to all areas of military and political affairs. It appears that major *successful* arms control will affect our relations with our potential enemies in ways that, on balance, would minimize the danger and occurrence of local war. (This is in addition to any direct arms-control measures oriented towards local war, including local wars among small powers.)

The same point can be made more concrete by noting that, while the danger of local war escalating into general war might be reduced, there is a new cost or risk that is introduced by a substantial arms-control agreement. That is the threat to the arms-control environment itself. For many reasons, direct and indirect, it seems likely that arms control may be vulnerable to the occurrence of local war, especially a violent one. One reason is simply that the atmosphere required for continuation of arms control may have been spoiled, and that both sides may recognize that the arms agreement will be a casualty in any significant war.

A second is that many of the arms controls or ancillary arrangements may be violated, or abandoned, as a necessary concomitant of fighting a war. Agreements regarding the use, disposition, production, or testing of nuclear weapons would be hard to maintain while a nuclear war was in process or during its aftermath. Inspection of military postures and movements might be intolerable in time of war. Some of the personnel exchanges involved in arms control might become politically intolerable; Russian and Chinese inspectors on American strategic-missile bases would be a genuine embarrassment during an attempted invasion of Formosa! Limits on the deployment of strategic forces, and especially the submission of strategic forces to surveillance, might be unacceptable if the danger of war rises above some threshold. And local war would raise it.

Of course, it can be argued that this is precisely the circumstance in which arms control is intended to work. If a main purpose of comprehensive limitations on strategic weapons is to make it less likely that inadvertent war will result in some crisis or arise from an escalation of limited war, the controls are presumably intended precisely for this contingency, and during normal times they are more in the nature of stand-by controls. But this does not contradict the proposition that to engage in local war is to risk the dismantlement of the arms control. It may be hoped and intended that the arms arrangements themselves will survive a crisis and prevent its getting worse; but if there is any uncertainty about how well it will work, or on which particular occasions it will work, it may induce caution.

It is also worth remarking that local war might be a deliberate cloak for clandestine evasion of arms control. All kinds of unusual activities might seem "justified" in a country that was busy with a local war; one expects unusual military communications, movements of military forces, intelligence activities, and so forth, to be a natural accompaniment of the domestic emergency that goes with an external war. This could either mean that a local war would be the means chosen for cloaking large scale evasions in the event evasions had already been decided on, or that those elements within a government that wished to bend or break certain limitations and rules would find the occurrence of local war a favorable opportunity for doing so.

There is no way to assess these various effects and reach a net conclusion even about whether local war will become a greater or lesser danger as a result of comprehensive arms control, unless some particular arms controls are specified. In addition, the question has much to do with the relation of China to both the Soviet Union and the arms arrangements. It also relates to the way arms limitations affect the solidarity or formation of alliances.

Cold War

Much of the discussion of arms control and local war can be applied more broadly to the relation between arms control and international strategy. On the one hand, arms control may be addressed directly to some of the instruments and capabilities for subversion, blackmail, intimidation, wars of nerves, and general international mischief; on the other hand, it may indirectly inhibit or facilitate certain kinds of aggressive or mischievous actions by suppressing some of the means to oppose them. By reducing the credibility of "massive retaliation," it may increase the credibility of lesser threats, including threats of limited aggression and limited retaliation. Weaker members of a loose alliance may feel even less protected than before. By quarantining local wars among small nations, it may make the world safer for the major powers but reduce the deterrence of small-power aggression.

These negative or discouraging remarks have to be made, because they are important considerations both in evaluating arms proposals and in assessing how disappointed we should be if arms control produces at least some aggravation of problems along with the benefits it may bring. These considerations also remind us that the strategic implications of any arms measures are complicated, and almost always are a mixture of advantages and disadvantages that have to be weighed. At the same time, it has to be emphasized that arms control need not aggravate these dangers disproportionately if we are alert to them in advance and can design measures in full knowledge that these problems exist. Arms control may have good effects and bad effects; "good" arms control will have fewer bad effects than "bad" arms control.

It should be repeated that to talk seriously about the implications of arms control, once achieved, is to talk about a situation in which certain political prerequisites have probably been met, prerequisites that may tend to reduce the likelihood of some of the most worrisome logical possibilities. And it would almost certainly be the case that a nation contemplating serious mischief would be aware that its actions could jeopardize the arms-control environment itself. While we are sometimes inclined to lament the fact that arms control, however durable its intent, is subject to breakdown and reversal, this very fragility of a breakable arrangement may have important deterrent effects. If the arms regulation is comprehensive enough or potent enough to make a genuine difference in the practice of international strategy, and if it is satisfactory enough in its over-all operation for the main participants to be willing to go along with it, the continuing threat, implicit or explicit, to throw it over or let it erode away if the performance of other countries is found unbearable, may have a powerful deterrent and disciplinary effect.

In other words, the threat to destroy the arrangement may be a potent one, potent for good or ill. It can be used to cajole and to intimidate aggressively, or it can be used to deter and to discipline potential mischief. Small nations may enhance their leverage in international affairs by behaving in a way that threatens to collapse the arms arrangements; they may also be deterred by the fear of success or by the pressure brought on them by other nations, perhaps small ones too, that cannot afford to see the arrangements collapse.

Chapter 7

EVASION, AVOIDANCE
AND BREAKDOWN

APART from the problems of interpreting and administering any agreement, there is the possibility of undetected evasion, of deliberate decisions to violate. Evading an agreement not to test megaton nuclear weapons aboveground might be nearly impossible, but for underground tests and smaller weapons — probably for most arms-control schemes — the possibility of evasion will be important. In assessing it, one must first have an estimate of the flaws in the inspection and intelligence process.

This estimate can only take the form of a statement of probabilities. If the agreement limits each side to some number of missiles, one asks the probability that one side could produce undetected an extra 20 missiles, an extra 50, an extra 200, and so on. The factors that go into this estimate are many, and include hidden stockpiles, clandestine production and assembly, and production of parts for assembling once the agreement breaks down. The form that the evasion takes would likely affect the evaluation of its consequences. The calculated probabilities will vary in reliability, depending on the nature of the agreement. Whether they imply that one should not enter the agreement depends largely, but not wholly, on the strategic implications of the agreement and of its evasion. Even if there were only small advantages to Russia from cheating on, say, a test moratorium, the United States might decide that for political reasons it should not willingly accept an agreement that establishes the principle of inadequate protection against evasion.

Second, it is necessary to assess the likelihood of the other's actually taking the chance. This would depend on the strategic value of cheating and also on how badly each side wanted the agreement to remain in force, and what each expected the other to do if it discovered cheating.

The critical factors will be the strategic implications. What does one gain by violating the agreement? What is gained by different kinds and amounts of cheating? A critical variable may be the permitted level of forces: the clandestine production of a score of missiles would have greater implications if the agreement banned all long-range delivery systems than if it permitted each side to have several hundred missiles. If both sides could readily hide 10 per cent of their present supply of fissionable material, an agreement reducing stockpiles to very low levels would be subject to large relative error and uncertainty.

Evaluation of cheating must consider three levels of conflict: general war, local war, and threats of war. Cheating would disturb the strategic balance insofar as it made it more likely that the evading nation could successfully attack the other's deterrent force. For a given number of weapons in an agreement, one can make (crude) estimates of how much either side would have to cheat to have a given probability of reducing the other side's retaliatory potency to a given level. (If one side is cheating and getting away with it, it will have to consider the possibility that the other is doing it too.)

An obvious form of cheating on a weapon limitation would be the production of clandestine weapons; in this case the object might be attack out of the blue. But evasion might be carried on in more subtle ways. One side might cheat on production of parts and components, then declare the agreement terminated — gaining a decisive lead in the resulting arms race. The potential head start from cheating is critical in assessing the problems of lead time and breakdown.

Cheating might have important consequences for local war. If evasion gave one side strategic dominance it might, rather than launch all-out war, use this as a cover under which to press limited aggression. Cheating on the tactical level may enable a country to develop more effective local-war forces. If one side cheats, for example, on an agreed level of fissionable material it may have tactical weapons to waste in a local war, while the other with the agreed minimum may be reluctant to expend it.

Cheating may affect opportunities for political blackmail. The side that cheats may not achieve enough advantage to launch a strategic attack, and may be unwilling to risk or initiate local war; nevertheless the resulting asymmetry may have important consequences. It should be noted, though, that the side that cheats may have to announce, or at least to make known, that it has done so. In fact, it may have to demonstrate it, in order to get the political leverage. A large supply of illicit weapons cannot be used for threats if they remain secret. (There is the interesting possibility that a nation may seek to convey the idea that it has cheated more than it actually has. This might be especially likely of smaller countries.) Thus the attempt to use illicit military force might involve renunciation of the agreement, or at least the admission that one has cheated. Hence the political advantages, though significant, may be effective only until others have caught up. During the interim the military advantage might be used effectively, particularly against third countries that recognized that they could not count on the protection of a superpower.

Evasion, then, can have very important effects on the military balance; but it cannot be assumed that an agreement that leaves some possibility of cheating is necessarily unacceptable or that cheating would necessarily result in important strategic gains.

Avoidance

Any arms control short of complete disarmament will permit the continuation of some military activities while eliminating others. Even in an arms-control environment, both sides will be concerned with defense and deterrence and will seek substitute (legal) methods and weapons to perform functions formerly dealt with by (now) prohibited methods and weapons.

"Avoidance" activities of this kind will fall into three general categories. First, there will be intended major alternative activities that are deemed more desirable. (Both sides might recognize that if the threat of massive retaliation is eliminated by an arms agreement, larger conventional forces may be needed; and both may prefer this.) Second, there will be major alternatives and loopholes in the agreement that are not anticipated, and which may nullify the intent of the agreement at added cost to both sides. Third, there will be marginal activities that, while foreseen, are impossible to rule out in the letter of an agreement either because they cannot be distinguished legally from permissible activities or because they cannot be defined precisely.

Major alterations in one's military position, designed to strengthen that position as much as possible within the agreement, have already been considered in relation to the strategic and limited-war balances. Here we need only point out that both sides inevitably will permit their military to carry on this kind of avoidance activity. In assessing the strategic implications of an agreement it is therefore necessary to anticipate what changes each side will make in its military forces. If missiles are banned, will better planes be developed? If so, will the arms agreement have accomplished its purpose, or will the military environment look more precarious? Or will it look the same with just more money being spent both to administer the agreement and to overcome it?

The assessment will require spelling out the specific reason behind limitations. If missiles were wanted to deter an enemy attack, but were produced "soft" (vulnerable) to save money or because the problem had not been thought through, then an agreement not to produce missiles vulnerable to megaton detonations a fraction of a mile away might be valuable, despite the obvious avoidance possibilities. The reason for the agreement would be to reduce the incentive to pre-empt; and this might be successfully accomplished even though there were avoidance. In some cases an agreement could serve to force military establishments to do what they should have done all along to gain maximum security but did not do for other reasons, perhaps because of the larger budgets required. Alternatively, an arms agreement might fail in its purpose if the avoidance activity is as dangerous as the activity denied, or more dangerous.

Loopholes and marginal activities involve a more technical and legal analysis, but have much of the same strategic implications. It should be anticipated that the military forces on both sides will be searching for ambiguities and loopholes. There would be serious morale problems in trying to get them not to or in resisting their efforts to take advantage of clear openings available to both sides.

If loopholes are left unplugged, the objectives of the control may not be obtained. The question must always be asked whether there are loopholes that we (or they) will feel tempted or obliged to exploit, and that will undermine the agreement. That some possibilities will be overlooked is an important reason for adjustment mechanisms in the agreement.

Breakdown

Arms agreements and understandings may terminate in a variety of ways. Some may be transient and run out; some may become obsolete technologically, and be dropped by mutual consent; some may have been tacit in the first place, and fade away or, upon a few contraventions, cease to obtain.

Formal agreements intended to be durable may break down in a number of ways. One side or both may denounce the agreement as no longer wise or justified, whether or not unilateral denunciation was envisaged as a legitimate mode of termination. Violations may become so rampant that the agreement ceases to be taken seriously, even though it remains nominally in effect. Secret violation may be discovered, or open violation may be embarked upon. And there may be specialized diplomacy and propaganda related to the breakdown of the agreement, each side trying to induce the other to incur responsibility for the breakdown, each accusing the other of hewing close to the letter of the agreement and violating the spirit, or one side arguing that the explicit conditions justifying termination have been met while the other is denying it.

An important question will be the interdependence of several understandings or agreements. Some limited agreements may erode or be destroyed, leaving others still in force; some may have the effect of symbolizing the breakdown of the whole formal arms-control effort. A "separability clause," so to speak, may insulate some agreements from the violation, denunciation, or abandonment of other agreements and restraints. The consequences of particular violations or the abandonment of particular understandings is a matter of uncertain judgment, not something to be inferred directly from the written instruments.

One must take into account the agreement's untimely breakdown through any of these modes and causes. One has to consider not only the strategic implications of the agreement itself, on the assumption it works, but the implications of an agreement that breaks down at any point in time and under any one of a number of possible circumstances. One also has to consider, in anticipating performance under the agreement, that the participants are likely to adapt themselves continually to the danger of untimely breakdown (or to the opportunities for it).

The problem of untimely breakdown arises most dramatically in considering a comprehensive arms limitation, one that drastically reduces military forces. This possibility has to be taken into account not only at the time the decision is made to proceed with the agreement but continually during the life of the agreement, because among the options available to any participant are denunciation and violation. It is unwise to expect any government to adhere long to the spirit and letter of an agreement that it has come to perceive as no longer compatible with its security interests. It has to be acknowledged that the motives for open violation, even clandestine violation, may be of the most respectable or of the most reprehensible sort. And the very likelihood that the other main participants, or the opposing bloc of participants, may at any time abandon the agreement is itself a motive for continually analyzing the wisdom of going along. There may, on the analogy with war itself, be a phenomenon of "preventive" or "pre-emptive" violation or denunciation.

The situation can be affected somewhat, but only somewhat, by the implicit or explicit understanding about the freedom of a participant to bolt the arrangement. There is probably no formal language that can quite make sudden denunciation appear immoral, irrespective of circumstances; and there is probably no permissive language that can quite dispel all moral inhibitions, or all propaganda losses, in invoking a clause that sanctions denunciation. In any event, the most urgent considerations of national security, even the highest motivations of international peace, may be involved in the decision to continue or not to continue abiding by the agreement; and all participating governments should be continually preoccupied with the policy question of whether, and just how, to stay within the agreement.

The possibility of an untimely resumption of the arms race should be a main consideration determining the content of the agreement itself. It was argued earlier that a very low level of strategic weapons might — whatever its advantages — be less stable than some higher level of weaponry on both sides. A related point is that the advantage that either side might achieve by suddenly breaking the agreement, getting a head start on the other, or by clandestinely violating it to the point where the secret could no longer be kept and then racing ahead in open violation, may be less if both sides begin from moderate levels of strategic weapons rather than from a position of real or imagined nakedness. One reason is that clandestine violation on any given scale — a scale whose upper limit is determined by the requirement of secrecy — will be less of a proportionate increase, and less of a threat to the other side, the higher the stockpile to which it is an increment. (A contrary consideration is that the violations may be more conspicuous, the lower the level of military production and activities permitted under the agreement.) A second reason is that a given increase in weaponry, achieved by a few months' head start in violation of the agreement, makes less difference if the deterrence is already reasonably stable.

Similarly, the sudden exploitation of some new technology may make less difference — be less of a temptation to the side that has it, and less cause for anxiety on the other — the greater the diversity of weapons allowed under the agreement.

It would be pushing the argument to an extreme to suggest that the present arms race is safer than an arms-control environment would be. Obviously there are countervailing considerations. The ones raised here have simply suggested that, other things equal, the risk of falling behind in a resumed arms race may be greater, the more drastic the disarmament out of which the arms race resumes.

The possibility of breakdown is an important reason why the stockpile of finished and ready weapons is by no means the main issue in a comprehensive program of arms limitation. The ready stockpile is mainly relevant to the possibility of surprise attack arising out of the agreement or out of clandestine violation. In modern strategic warfare, the "mobilization base" can make very little difference to the course of the war once it has started. But the production base for the resumption of the arms race may be all-important in a resumed arms race. Productive capacity, stockpiles of components, weapons in process of production, a reserve of trained crews, and the convertibility of permitted weapons to un-permitted forms, are what may determine who "wins" the arms race if it is resumed.

Thus in considering how one is making out under the arms agreement one must consider, so to speak, what the balance of forces would be at various intervals after the arms race were resumed, on various assumptions about the degree to which the resumption had been anticipated openly or clandestinely on both sides.

These remarks may sound cynical and pessimistic. But there is another interpretation of the subject. It is that a comprehensive program of arms limitation is essentially a mutual-warning agreement, by which both sides get into such positions that they could achieve dominant military postures only by unilaterally taking actions that would be unmistakenly visible. To say that any arms agreement may end in an arms race is to say that a comprehensive arms agreement may make it impossible to embark upon final preparations for war without signaling one's intentions. In addition, if it is clear that the scale and intensity of activity required, upon breaking the agreement, to achieve a dominant military position could be quickly perceived and responded to by the other side, the result may be that nobody can clearly "win" the ensuing arms race. There is less temptation, then, to embark on it.

From this point of view, to consider openly the possibility that either side would bolt the agreement and dash for supremacy is not incompatible with the spirit of disarmament. Rather, to do so is to focus on a main criterion for the arms reduction. The criterion is that the level of armaments and — perhaps even more important — the short-run and long-run arms-race potential of the participants should be at such levels and at such ratios as to make it exceedingly unlikely that either could gain a clear lead over the other. To state the criterion is not to make it an easy one to apply, especially in a world of drastic and unexpected changes in technology. But it does seem certain that the strategic evaluation of the potential arms race that may ensue upon breakdown of the agreement is on a par with the strategic evaluation of the agreed limitations themselves, and no less legitimate a subject for study and discussion.

PART III

MAKING ARMS CONTROL WORK

PART II

Chapter 8

BARGAINING
AND AGREEMENT

Aʀᴍs control is customarily thought of as entailing formal agreements, negotiated in detail at diplomatic conferences, embodied in a treaty, and with machinery or institutions for monitoring the agreement. But a more variegated and flexible concept of arms control is necessary — one that recognizes that the degree of formality may range from a formal treaty with detailed specifications, at one end of the scale, through executive agreements, explicit but informal understandings, tacit understandings, to self-restraint that is consciously contingent on each other's behavior.

Formal vs. Informal Understandings

The essence of arms control is some kind of mutual restraint, collaborative action, or exchange of facilities between potential enemies in the interest of reducing the likelihood of war, the scope of war if it occurs, or its consequences. It is an important tactical question whether the most promising approach to arms control is to seek formal treaties, informal agreements, tacit understandings, or just mutual self-restraint; there are many points of view on this, and much to be said for and against each of them. If a formal agreement helps to identify areas of potential mutual restraint or cooperation, and facilitates understandings by which both sides may restrain their actions, it contributes to arms control. But it is not the formal agreement or treaty itself that constitutes arms control; mutual restraints that can be reached without explicit negotiation

77

are no less relevant to the subject of this book just because they lack some of the diplomatic trappings.

To emphasize this point, which is far too little appreciated, it may help to recognize that limited war itself is a form of arms control, and one that customarily has not been arrived at by explicit negotiation and formal agreements. A "limited arms race" may not be wholly different in character from limited war, in the sense that it may stem from an appreciation on both sides that there are advantages in abstaining from certain unilateral military actions as long as the other does too, and that these can often be perceived, and limits arrived at, without benefit of full communication and overtly acknowledged agreement. As already indicated, there are many unilateral military actions that both we and the Soviets abstain from at the present time, out of what must certainly be a recognition that the game is dangerous if both play it, and both can play the game; most of these "traffic rules" and rules of privacy are quite informal.*

But the fact that understandings can be quite informal, and that this possibility deserves emphasis, does not imply that they are necessarily preferable when the alternative of a formal agreement is open.

To some extent, the formality of the understanding reached will depend on the contents of the understanding. It may take no formal instrument at all to support an understanding to abstain from certain blatant kinds of mischief; it is bound to require a formal undertaking if each side grants, say, real estate and privileged personnel to the other, and shares some of the costs. In general, exchanges of facilities, or the undertaking of activity on each other's soil, or the sharing of costs, require formal agreements and institutions, and might be called "positive" or "active" arms control. The more "passive" kind, involved in simply abstaining from certain activities, or in noninterference with the other side's surveillance or intelligence activities, may possibly benefit from explicit understandings but does not necessarily require them. Again, restraints and traffic rules and understandings that have evolved over time and have become

---

* For further discussion of "informal" rules, limits, and controls on arms and their use, see T. C. Schelling, "Reciprocal Measures for Arms Stabilization," *Daedalus* LXXXIX (Fall 1960) 892–914, and Roger D. Fisher, "Constructing Rules that Affect Governments," to appear in Donald G. Brennan (ed.) *Arms Control, Disarmament, and National Security.*

"traditions" perhaps need no formal expression, and may sometimes even be demoralized by efforts to reduce them to detailed and explicit terms; new restraints, or restraints in the conduct of a novel activity, may lack the benefit of tradition and require a more expeditious means of reaching an agreement.

There is undoubtedly some correlation between the comprehensiveness of the arms control that one seeks and the degree of formality appropriate to the negotiations and the agreement. Certainly a very comprehensive limitation on weapons and their deployment is likely to require a good deal of governmental machinery for its enforcement, inspection, adaptation, and general housekeeping. Undoubtedly, also, arms control that is part of a program to provide alternative ways of settling disputes, to establish a system of world law or of world legislation, especially to create institutions for international enforcement, and to reduce national responsibilities for policing the world against violence, is almost necessarily committed to the creation of formal institutions. Arms control that is more opportunistic or limited in its intent, that seeks to supplement national military policies in directions that are mutually beneficial but that has no ambitious expectations of directly revising national responsibility or of drastically altering the basically national orientation of military or diplomatic policy, does not necessarily involve formal undertakings and formal institutions.

The difference between collaborative action and mutual restraint is pertinent here. In a sense, the kinds of mischief of a military or quasi-military sort that nations might engage in are virtually infinite. The things that we may agree with other nations to engage in are necessarily finite and limited, while a list of the things that we may implicitly commit ourselves to refrain from under a general understanding about good behavior is potentially as long as the devil himself could make it. But to strike an analogy, what goes into a collective-bargaining agreement are mainly the things that both sides will do for each other: the wages, working hours, fringe benefits, rest periods, vacations, health and sanitation facilities to be provided, and so forth. The number of ways that a mischievous worker could damage the employer's interests must be unlimited; but the agreement does not find it necessary to list them all, since an implicit "good behavior" commitment is taken for granted. By the same token, anti-mischief arms control could probably never be explicit and comprehensive, if only because types of mischief could be invented just as rapidly as they can be written down.

A closely related issue is that of whether an agreement, formal or informal, will be detailed and explicit in its terms, or vague and general. There are at least two questions here. One is, how feasible it is to define in advance all the contingencies that may arise under the agreement, and all of the relevant interpretations, in fine detail. The second is, whether, if that is possible, it is wise to put them all in the agreement. The same problem arises with legislation; some of our most potent and far-reaching laws, like those against combinations in restraint of trade, as well as some of the most potent clauses of our constitution, are broad, general, somewhat vague, subject to interpretation in particular instances, and dependent on the subsequent accumulation of some coherent body of "case law," or interpretations. Other legislation is quite detailed and explicit. There is much to be said for both types, and in fact an enormous amount has been said, even with respect to international agreements; but arms control may be a sufficiently distinctive field of activity to require more thought on the matter.

Communicating with the Potential Enemy (Partner)

Even in the case of formal diplomatic negotiation, culminating in a treaty, communicating with the partner (potential enemy) country is a complex matter. In addition to the deliberate formal and informal communications (public and private) coordinated by the head of government, there is a good deal of activity designed to impress the other side with the firmness of one's own position, the pressures that one is subject to, and the areas in which one is willing to make concessions. Furthermore, especially in a democratic country, there is no single "government" with a single voice; there are separate branches of government, each one of which embodies a variety of unreconciled differences and interests. America speaks to Russia not only through its ambassadors, but through Senators and Congressmen of both parties, through pressure groups and lobbyists, through columnists and scholars. The executive branch itself consists of cabinet members who have strongly different interests, all of whom hold press conferences in which they both deliberately and inadvertently convey some notion of what one should expect this country to agree to, insist on, think of, and propose. We speak, furthermore, not only to the countries we negotiate with, but to allied countries and neutral countries, with intentional or unintentional conveyance to our potential enemies of correct or incorrect notions of what our position is.

Negotiating informal understandings is an even more diffuse activity. In all cases, actions speak loudly, whether or not more loudly than words; to change the defense budget, to go on airborne alert, to switch from fixed-based to mobile missiles, to withdraw troops from particular areas, to sign treaties and to make arrangements with particular countries, are ways of communicating intentions, expectations, values and commitments, to our potential enemies. However formal the negotiations, much of our communication is in the form of our actions, whether we so intend it or not. In very informal communication, especially in the kind of tacit bargaining that goes on continuously between us and the Soviets, actions rather than words may carry even more of the burden. Indirect discourse carries even more of the burden too, and press conferences, inspired leaks, hints to third countries, and so forth, are all part of the communication process.*

Consider, for example, how we communicate to the Russians our proposal regarding the use of nuclear weapons in the event of limited war. The way we equip our armed forces and the training they are given are main ways we communicate our intentions to the enemy. The way we deploy nuclear weapons and centralize or decentralize control of nuclear weapons (to the extent that they can be discerned and appreciated by the enemy) are other ways. The statements of executive-branch and Congressional leaders directed not towards the Soviets but towards appropriations committees, towards the American public, and towards allied countries are sources of communication with the potential enemy. Even silence is a mode of communication; failure to deny rumors, refusal to answer questions, attempts to take emphasis away from certain issues, all tend to communicate something to the enemy. In some cases the communication is of reasonably high fidelity; in other

* The following excerpt from *The New York Times* of October 14, 1960, regarding the prospective launching of the "Samos" photographic satellite, illustrates the point. "United States officials will be watching for the reaction of the Soviet Government to the launching. In the present nebulous and formative state of space law, the Soviet reaction will become an important guide in establishing national and international rights in space." (p. 12.)

cases it is inadvertent but nevertheless revealing or confusing; in other cases it is deliberately confusing; in other cases it may be deliberately deceptive. But all of these actions and statements and inactions and silences convey something to the Soviets about the circumstances in which we would use nuclear weapons, how we would use them, for what purposes, and in what quantities.

Our attitudes towards arms control, and our concrete ideas on the subject of arms control, also get communicated in this variety of ways. Our "negotiations" with the Soviets over the past several years have not been solely those that took place in Geneva, or at the United Nations in New York, or in exchanges of letters between Presidents and Premiers. Our communications have been of all the sorts mentioned above. Furthermore, there may be a problem of educating the countries with which we may want to reach arms understandings. If indeed we have ideas about the kinds of arms control that may be most promising, and about the relation of arms control to our military policy, the problem may be not only one of communicating these ideas as proposals to the Soviets, but also one of showing the Soviets that these are reasonable ideas, that they correspond to a sensible and logical arms-control conception, that they are sensible enough that we might take them seriously, and that perhaps they should too. In other words, persuasion may be required; and the channels of persuasion may include a number of informal and unofficial media. In order to do this successfully we need to know a great deal more than we now do about Soviet attitudes towards arms control, their perception of American intentions, and their negotiating methods.

Modes of Negotiation

Techniques of negotiation in the field of arms control deserve imaginative study. Negotiating with an actual or potential enemy on important security measures is not quite the same as negotiating trade agreements, diplomatic immunities, or even political settlements. For one thing, military secrecy is importantly involved; a nation is understandably reluctant, for example, in opening negotiations on schemes to discourage surprise attack, to identify for the enemy precisely those points at which it is most vulnerable. Second, in military intelligence, a special kind of secrecy problem is also involved; arms arrangements and even discussions of arms arrangements impinge on varieties of clandestine activities that the participants engage in, and many forms of arms control are directly related to gaps in the participants' military intelligence of each other. Third, extraordinarily complicated technical military and engineering problems are likely to be critically involved in any arms negotiation; and while it is undoubtedly true that political settlements, tax arrangements, status-of-forces agreements, and international monetary arrangements involve intricate technical questions, it is probably a fair observation that arms negotiations involve more, or at least involve technical problems of the kind that are less familiar to professional diplomats and negotiators. It is probably also true that the essential technical information in the military field changes more rapidly, and is therefore much more difficult to keep up to date, than most political and economic data.

Finally, any serious arms arrangement would involve matters of extreme importance to governments; and while arms control is not unique in its involvement of vital national considerations, it at least occupies the same end of the scale with political negotiations of the highest importance, so that the cost involved in mismanagement, in lost opportunities, in inadvertent commitments, or in agreements mistakenly arrived at, cannot readily be taken in stride as just ordinary ups and downs of international diplomacy. This is vital business.

The problem of coordinating expert military and engineering judgment with diplomatic negotiation is therefore more difficult, and undoubtedly more important, than the problem of incorporating expert industrial and engineering judgment in negotiations on, say, commodity stabilization. Evidence of the importance of this problem, and of the fact that it has not been adequately solved, is in the attempts, not altogether successful, of distinguishing between "technical discussion" and "political negotiations" in the test-ban and surprise-attack negotiations of the last few years. Whatever the value of the so-called "technical discussions," it is perfectly clear that their meaning and their purpose were not a matter of full agreement and common understanding between East and West. And it is almost as clear that, whatever the value of drawing a line between technical and political exchanges, the line is not an easy one to draw even with the best of intentions.

Certainly it would be naive to suppose that any technical discussions between East and West on arms-control questions could occur without importantly involving the bargaining positions, the commitments, and the political expectations of both sides. Just to acknowledge that certain technical questions are worth discussing can be of genuine bargaining significance; and the criteria by which one evaluates certain technical possibilities or technical risks must relate to fundamental political and military decisions. It may, for example, in a particular case seem to be a purely "technical" question what the probability is that a particular attack could succeed, or that a particular violation would go undetected, just as it may be a purely technical question what the increased probability of airplane accidents would be if certain safety standards were relaxed. But whether these probabilities are trivially small or intolerably large is a matter of fundamental political and military evaluation. So the possibility of conducting important technical discussions that are wholly sterilized against any possible "political" implications seems to be zero.

This does not mean that the institution of "technical discussion" is not useful. It means only that we should not pretend that the distinction is entirely clean, that pure technicians uninstructed politically can conduct the technical discussions on their own, and that no political commitments are taken when agreement is reached to proceed with technical discussions in a particular area. Technical discussions can be substantively important in a political setting. And, quite possibly, the pretense of technical discussion may help to reduce the sense of political commitment, even though it cannot hope to eliminate it, and prove a useful means of reaching "political" understandings.

Other negotiating techniques may deserve further study, too. The role of mediators, for example, deserves to be carefully considered. It is evidently true in the field of arms control, as in almost any other field, that an agreement could be crystallized, or a compromise acknowledged by both sides, if only there were some noncommittal way of getting the appropriate proposal made. Often each side is afraid of making a concession for fear that the other will expect capitulation. Often each side finds it politically embarrassing to be the first to back down. Often one or both sides would acquiesce in an agreement if the agreement did not seem to correspond too closely to the other side's latest favorite position. In these circumstances, the mediator or conciliator who exercises a power of suggestion, and who has the ability to take responsibility for proposals that neither of the main participants can bring himself to make, can perform an important service. At least this is true of those cases in which a tenuous agreement exists *de facto*, and can be strengthened by some process of acknowledgment. Even the mere assertion of a statement of affairs by a skilled mediator can, through the absence of overt contradiction by the main participants, create a feeling that the matter is settled. At least this may be true of those forms of arms control that involve simple understandings of how to abstain from certain actions, rather than elaborate schedules and procedures for collaboration. Perhaps the main participants, the U.S. and the U.S.S.R., can even profitably cultivate certain mediators in the field of arms control. This might be particularly relevant to those forms of arms control that involve important, but not quite vital, issues.

Other techniques of negotiation, ranging from "summit" conferences and U.N. debates to the use of interviews by journalists, deserve to be considered. What is particularly important to keep in mind is that the significance of any of these modes of negotiation is not to be judged solely by the signed or ratified document that may emerge to record an explicit agreement, but also by whether certain rules, restraints, traditions, better understandings or cooperative actions result from the negotiations, even in the absence of any formal success embodied in official documents. Understandings reached, bargains struck, inhibitions created, and agreements crystallized, as an apparent by-product of negotiations, may well be more important than the particular agreement that is reached or not reached in the formal negotiations.

Publicity and Secrecy

A special aspect of negotiation, and even of the understandings reached, is the matter of secrecy or publicity. Perhaps "privacy" vs. publicity is a better expression in some cases. Certainly there may be advantages in reducing the propaganda significance of negotiations, by prior agreement on privacy, on not making a record of negotiations public, on not holding separate press conferences to give away one's own view of what is going on. There is also the important possibility that the main participants in arms control negotiations are embarrassed and inhibited by the presence of allied countries or countries to which they have military commitments. Secrecy may eliminate some of the obstacles to plain speaking and to drastic proposals. Secrecy may also be involved in negotiating matters that one or both participants prefer not to acknowledge in public.

Finally, there is the possibility of secret agreements, as well as of secret negotiations. Agreements, for example, regarding the conduct of clandestine intelligence, or the cessation of intrusions, spoofing activity, harassment, and so forth might have to be secret only because the matters discussed are usually not openly acknowledged. If our definition of arms controls is broad enough to include all the possible forms of military collaboration between the United States and its main enemies, there may well be understandings reached, or even explicit agreements, that must be kept from certain other countries. For example, agreements about preventing the spread of weapon technology, or even of nuclear weapons, or agreements involving delicate political settlements, might well have to remain secret. The peculiar status of relations between the U.S.S.R. and China is a potent reminder that we are not the only major country that may occasionally wish to be less than wholly candid with its allies.

Content of Agreements

For those kinds of arms controls that require, or make desirable, an explicit and formal agreement, there are nevertheless important questions about how much of the understanding can be, or should be, detailed in the agreement itself and how much of the understanding left out. There is also the interesting question of how much *misunderstanding* may be incorporated unrecognized into the agreement, and how much misunderstanding may be knowingly tolerated by the signatories. It seems perfectly clear that, for an agreement that is anything but a general statement of common interest and intent, it is impossible to nail everything down in an exhaustively explicit agreement, leaving no details subject to subsequent interpretations and misinterpretations, leaving no issues unresolved, leaving no intentions inarticulate, and leaving no circumstances unanticipated. An arms-control agreement, like any other contract or piece of legislation, would require subsequent interpretation and negotiation and would undoubtedly discover omissions and misunderstandings in the course of its operation. In other words, it is bound to be essentially incomplete, as almost any agreement is.

Unlike other fields in which contracts are regularly made, or diplomatic negotiations regularly occur, the field of arms control enjoys no accumulated body of precedents, of "case law," capable of supplying interpretations, filling the omissions and guiding the subsequent negotiations. This is not like a real estate transaction in which a brief purchase agreement can include, by reference, a great mass of local and general law and custom.

As with other laws and contracts, including laws and contracts in novel areas, it is not necessarily true that every effort should be made to make the agreement as detailed as possible and to anticipate as many contingencies as one can. While it is important on the one hand to incorporate as much as possible of the understanding in a written document to preclude further misunderstandings, it is also important to avoid freezing detailed answers to very dimly perceived questions in a document that is supposed to guide the participants in their relations to each other through fairly uncharted territory. It may also be important to reach agreement early rather than late, and not to hold up agreement pending the exhaustive exploration of all its possible implications by the participants.

These comments are supported by the fact that the technical and military details of an arms agreement might be subject to very rapid obsolescence — so rapid that negotiators, trying to catch up with most recent developments to incorporate them into the agreement itself, may fall further and further behind in the attempt.

Given that the agreement is bound to be incomplete, and that it may not even be wise to try to make it as complete as possible, there is an important question whether the agreement should set up procedures and institutions for its own interpretation and subsequent evolution.

An interesting question is how much consensus is likely to be reached on the spirit and intent of an agreement. One of the things that makes it possible to get laws passed in a country like the United States is that people can agree on what to do and what not to do without having to agree on the motives and purposes. Certainly the discussion of the nuclear-test ban illustrates that a variety of motives can bring an issue to the point where agreement on some act, or on abstention of some act, is a live possibility, without any agreement among the participants as to the motives, and without even any consensus within some of the individual participating countries on the relative emphasis to be given different motives.

Furthermore, any arms agreement would be part of a broader political and military context, and part of the continuous process of diplomacy, propaganda, political relations and military maneuver, and would therefore impinge on a number of vital activities that are themselves not part of the agreement and on which there is no pretense of a consensus in spirit. It may very likely be perfectly clear, at the time an agreement is signed, that there is substantial remaining disagreement on the importance to be accorded to the agreement so far reached on what other measures may follow, and on what kind of relationship among the participants is assumed to be compatible with the agreement itself.

For example, agreement on a nuclear-test ban could be interpreted as a first step towards further arms control, or as the last step in a particular political maneuver. It could be interpreted to mean that weapon tests were over, and that is all, or to mean that nuclear weapons will henceforth be regarded, even more than before, as peculiarly different weapons, weapons peculiarly subject to restraint, weapons whose psychological status is different from that of high explosives.

There is probably some difference between agreements that require positive action from the participants, and agreements that involve restraint and abstention, in so far as related activities may be covered implicitly. As remarked earlier, the kinds of mischief that nations might do in a military or quasi-military way are unlimited and could not be exhaustively specified. Nevertheless, a general agreement not to engage in mischief, or a specific agreement banning a number of identified types of mischief, would imply a prohibition against a variety of actions upon which most of the participants might have a substantially common judgment. Nevertheless, it remains an act of judgment to determine whether certain forms of, say, intelligence activity, propaganda activity, military maneuver, and so forth are or are not implicitly covered by an agreement that, while it fails to specify them, clearly was intended to cover more than it could specify.

Interrelation with International Political Issues and Negotiations

It has been a central assumption of this book that some explicit as well as implicit arms agreements are possible without the prior settlement of major political issues. But not all potential forms of arms control are possible without political settlements. Some arms agreements inherently involve political settlements; and in some cases the arms aspect of the agreement may be relatively insignificant.

Disengagement in Europe, while it would clearly involve arms control, also must deal with a number of important political issues. The Austrian peace treaty pledging Austria to neutrality is essentially a political document; but the outlawing of a possible military alliance is a significant part of the arrangement. Although agreements of this kind are clearly important parts of the arms-control spectrum they are not discussed in detail at any stage of this book. We are concerned primarily with the military functions of arms control and with the strategic implications of agreements whose primary function is military.

Nevertheless, any arms agreement will have repercussions in the international political arena. The military-political implications of arms agreements have been discussed above. Here we are concerned with the interaction of arms-control negotiations with political issues and bargaining.

Even negotiations that are concerned primarily (or "exclusively") with military activities will have to deal with political issues. What countries are invited to the negotiations, where and when they are held, whether under U.N. auspices or not, what negotiating process is used — all of these are important political questions which have continually plagued disarmament negotiations. The Soviet campaign for equal representation of East and West at all international conferences has carried over to disarmament negotiations, and the acceptance by the West of the Committee of Ten for the Geneva negotiations in the summer of 1960 established a precedent which may have important implications for future *political* negotiations. Whether or not the United Nations machinery is used for arms negotiations can have important implications for the prestige of the U.N. and hence its effectiveness in other areas.

Not only are political implications inexorably bound up with any arms-control negotiations, but some of the details of an agreement are likely to have similar implications. The most outstanding of these has been the question of the role of Red China both in the negotiations and in the implementing of any agreement. In the test-ban negotiations it has been widely assumed that Red China would have to be brought into any working agreement. It is clear that whatever the final settlement of this question (if one is reached) it will have political implications beyond the agreement. In addition to the question of what countries participate there are a number of other factors of political importance including the role projected for the United Nations. Finally, one should not rule out the possibility of, in effect, joining arms control and political negotiations in a way that makes possible agreement in both.

Chapter 9

INSPECTION

AND INFORMATION

INSPECTION has been overemphasized in most discussions of arms control. It is but one of a series of problems involved in making arms control work. The problem is by no means as simple as catching a crook and convicting him; and, if it were, the role of information gathering would still be subtle and complex.

Much of the confusion has come from a failure to distinguish several different problems. First, what is the system of inspection and examination that an agreement should explicitly establish? Second, how much do we need to know about enemy compliance with the particular limits, restraints, and programs provided in the agreement? Third, what kind of evidence do we need in order to confront suspected violators, or to prove a case before third parties who have formal responsibility or a general interest in the matter? Fourth, what is the over-all role of inspection, interrogation, and intelligence gathering in keeping ourselves assured throughout the life of the agreement that the agreement itself and the participants' behavior are consistent with our maintaining the agreement?

These questions overlap but none quite contains another. The first, regarding the particular system of inspection and examination that the agreement might provide for, would appear to be the most limited. The agreed inspection is only part of the intelligence system that we would rely on — though an essential part in many cases.* Nevertheless, while the central function of inspection is to

* For a discussion of techniques useful in the inspection of various types of arms agreements see Bernard T. Feld, "Inspection Techniques of Arms Control," *Daedalus* LXXXIX (Fall 1960) 860–78.

get information we need, there could be reasons for providing in the formal system for types of information that we do not need for the evaluation of our security. We might wish to demand inspection in areas in which our unilateral intelligence is already adequate, in order not to demonstrate where our intelligence is adequate and where it is not.

We may also wish to utilize inspection procedures as part of the informal business of discussing and negotiating with each other, and identifying potential disputes before they become too serious. Formal inspection procedures frequently involve continual consultation and negotiation; they provide a channel of discussion and communication that is less dramatic and high-level than would be involved in overt charges of violation. They may help in general to normalize a mutual supervisory relationship that is otherwise in danger of becoming too sensitive and dramatic. Provisions for periodic reports and disclosures serve not only the purpose of providing information but of providing an occasion and a technique of continual low-level interrogation and negotiation.

In addition, the systems of inspection associated with an arms agreement may anticipate subsequent agreements, providing a base from which more extensive inspection or consultation could be extended. This might be explicitly agreed on by both sides; it might be anticipated by one and not the other; or it might be tacitly recognized, but not explicitly negotiated because of the unreadiness of one or both to reach agreement on what they foresee for the future.

The second question — what we need to know or to verify about the other side's *compliance with the agreement* — is commonly considered the main or sole focus of inspection. This is a faulty notion. An agreement to limit a particular weapon or its mode of deployment can substantially increase the importance of keeping other activities — activities not explicitly covered by the agreement — under better surveillance. An agreement limiting missiles, for example, will enhance each side's concern about the other's air force. Limitations on particular weapons may enhance each side's interest in the other's research and development of new weapons.

In general, then, the impact of a particular arms limitation on both sides' requirements for intelligence is *not* limited to the question of compliance with the particular limitations imposed.

The evidence question is still different. It is one thing to "know" that something is going on; it is another to persuade one's allies, or some judicial body or world opinion, the suspected violator, or even ourselves, that we have reliable evidence. The agreement itself may establish procedures and criteria that specify what kinds of evidence are admissible or what kinds are grounds for invoking special investigative activities. Evidence obtained through clandestine channels may also be too sensitive to reveal. And while each nation may have a good idea of the reliability of its own sources of intelligence, it may be unable to persuade other parties; what to one country's authorities is a responsible eyewitness account, to another country is simply hearsay. Governments must consider whether they can persuade even their own populations, their own press or legislature, or their own political opposition, that their allegations of violation are valid and responsible. This will particularly be the case when the evidence is imperfect, and requires a judgment of the likelihood that willful or inadvertent violation has occurred.

Finally, there is the broad question of the over-all role of inspection and intelligence in assuring ourselves that the arms limitations are consistent with our security. The inspection provided for within the agreement, together with other means of observation and surveillance, play a broader and more dynamic role than detecting violations. They must continually help to safeguard against the threat of attack and the fear of attack; they must continually provide valid reassurance against the danger of war, premeditated or accidental. The information obtained by the formal inspection system will be channeled into the regular intelligence collating and evaluating procedure and treated as a piece of data of some, but not complete, reliability. Inspection and intelligence must also continually verify the basic premises underlying the arms-limitation agreement, as the arms-control plan unfolds. Each side's expectations about the kinds and numbers of weapons on the other side and their location, the weapons under development, the vulnerabilities of weapons and communications, the reliability of communication and control systems, and the intelligence available to both sides, are likely to change as the arms agreement goes into effect; and the agreement itself must be continuously evaluated in the light of the strategic picture that emerges from the inspection and the intelligence activities.

Furthermore, each side's adaptations to whatever understandings are reached, or whatever limitations are agreed on, could not be entirely foretold in advance; inspection and surveillance must serve to keep each side informed of significant military developments that may require modifications in the agreement or supplementary understandings, or that entail reciprocal action on both sides.

Two Types of Error

Surveillance is bound to be imperfect, even when supplemented by all sources of information, clandestine and other. The practical criterion is not whether there is absolute safeguard against transgression, but how good the safeguards are. This is true of the efficacy of the system in *deterring* violation, through the expectation that violation would be caught and penalized, or of its efficacy in *discovering* violation so that countermeasures can be taken. But it is essential to recognize that an imperfect system can err in two directions.

It can cause us to miss violations, preparations for violation, or the fruits of past violation by the other side. But it can also produce mistaken evidence that a violation has occurred. Nearly all of the attention given to the inspection problem, notably with respect to the test ban in recent months, revolves around the possibility that the enemy may cheat without our knowing it or being able to prove it. Remarkably little attention is given to the serious danger that one side or the other will have, or think it has, evidence that the other is cheating when in fact it is not.

The importance of minimizing "false positives" as well as "false negatives" can hardly be exaggerated, particularly since there is a tendency to neglect it. The problem is not solely that of protecting the innocent — a problem we take for granted in the enforcement of domestic laws — although even this deserves some consideration. (Not all of the possible violators will be countries whose underlying motives we have reason to suspect.) The problem is also one of keeping the arms agreement from exacerbating tensions, suspicions, and international irritations with false alarms.

Furthermore, the intensive examination of evidence of possible violation will be unmanageable if the system is swamped with false alarms. And a participant can disguise his actual violation if our surveillance is so beset with false and ambiguous evidence that we learn to ignore the warning bells. Finally, it is important not to degrade the deterrent value of our surveillance by a system that leads participants to believe they are going to be accused and suspected anyway, and may as well violate for all the difference it would make.

There is a tendency for the two kinds of reliability of a surveillance system — that is, for the two kinds of error — to compete with each other. This is especially true of systems in which there is some rule or criterion for the selection of evidence, such as the frequency with which a particular activity is observed, or the background activity to be considered normal, or the sensitivity of the procedures or instrumentation to suspicious activities. The test ban provides a good illustration. If we generously suppose that earthquakes will be large and frequent, and overlook them unless very large ones appear with suspicious frequency, our system will rarely give false alarms but is in danger of missing violations. If we go to the other extreme and conservatively take small perturbations to be suspicious evidence, we may overburden the system and build up an enormous body of incriminatory evidence against both sides. Wherever the line is drawn, it has to represent a balance between these opposing kinds of error.

Nor is this just a matter of maintaining civil relations and avoiding nominal evidence of suspicious behavior. Even in our own analysis we want to avoid believing that violation has occurred if it has not. It will be expensive for us if we are continually preparing for the consequences of assumed violation when we might have known better. And the arms arrangements themselves will be jeopardized if we or any other participant has exaggerated notions of how much violation is occurring. Our willingness to continue, to negotiate more agreements, and to resist violating it or denouncing it ourselves, is at stake. And surely we don't want to encourage potential enemy countries to violate in "self-defense" in the mistaken belief that we have already violated.

The Voluntary-Evidence Principle

It is widely assumed that the specific rights of inspection, and facilities for inspection, that go with an arms arrangement should be provided in the arrangement itself — aside from the ordinary intelligence, clandestine and other, that countries expect to continue. But it may be better to consider the inspection provided in the agreement itself to be only a minimum. Supposing that each side will comply and wishes the other to know it, we ought to assume that each country is motivated to provide *sufficient* evidence, not just to submit to the agreed examination.

Actually this principle might be carried to the point of providing no inspection at all in the agreement. There is nothing illogical about an arms limitation based on the principle that each side has to be continually assured that the other is complying, and that it is the responsibility of each to demonstrate compliance in any way that it can. Each would go along with the agreement only as long as it was assured beyond reasonable doubt that the other's performance was satisfactory; and it would be up to each to invite such examination, and to extend such facilities, as would leave no reasonable doubt. Such a philosophy would be a dramatic reminder that the prime condition for continuation of the arrangement is that each be genuinely satisfied by the evidence the other provides.

This would be an extreme philosophy, involving difficulties of its own. It could be abused by each side's insisting that it harbored suspicions and needed more and more facilities and information. But the principle is sound and will underlie almost any arms agreement. The principle is simply that we need the assurance, and they need the assurance, that the agreement is being complied with to a reasonable degree and beyond reasonable doubt. Whatever inspection has been agreed on, if it is inadequate it is in the interest of both sides, the host as well as the examiner, to make up the deficiency and get across the evidence needed to keep both sides satisfied.

The principle will also undoubtedly be involved with respect to the intelligence facilities that both sides take for granted independently of the agreement. Surely not all the sources of information would be specified in the agreement; and an unwritten rule would be that participating countries not abuse the system by closing down the kinds of access that were taken for granted. But here, only some rule of reason could be applied.

Furthermore, almost any inspection scheme will prove deficient in some respects. In other respects it may prove onerous to the host country, even though no difficulties were foreseen. Demands for more information, and proposals to give up certain rights that proved burdensome but unnecessary, would be part of the ordinary business of making the agreement work. There is room for excessive demands and excessive denials, whether or not both sides originally thought that they had specified in detail exactly what was subject to examination.

For that reason it is worth while to emphasize, in this book but also in arms negotiations themselves, that the fundamental responsibility for the provision of adequate information lies with the host country.

Another point should be kept in mind. The more detailed and specific the agreement is on the rights of inspection and the facilities to be granted, the more it may seem to limit inspection and facilities to what is specified. It is not necessarily true that the more inspection is specified the more complete will be the coverage. It may be as important, or more important, to see that the right philosophy is emphasized: that each side has a fundamental interest in persuasively demonstrating its own compliance.

The Positive-Evidence Principle

There are two different criteria for judging inspection systems. One is how well the system gets at the truth in spite of the subject's best efforts to conceal it; the other is how well it helps the subject to display the truth when it is in his interest to do so. The difference is a little like that between a scheme for discovering the guilty and a scheme for permitting the innocent to establish their innocence.

To some extent, the difference is between an inspection scheme for discovering what the other country *is* doing, and a scheme to facilitate the other country's demonstrating what it is *not* doing. To search a million square miles of ocean or sky to assure oneself that no unauthorized submarines or aircraft are in the area could be enormously difficult and expensive, or impossible. But if the submarines or aircraft in question can be displayed in a way that makes clear where they *are*, we automatically know where they are *not*. This requires that the country whose forces are causing the concern be willing to take positive steps to give us the direct knowledge we need. And this principle assumes that each side, if it is *not* violating the understanding, or if it is *not* preparing to launch an attack, is motivated to demonstrate the fact.

It is this motivation on which the success of any arms inspection may ultimately rest. If we are in fact complying with an agreement, we badly wish to prove so; and if the other countries are genuinely complying with the spirit and letter of the agreement, they have every reason to want full credit for it. It is in this contingency — the contingency that the participants in fact are complying with the agreement and are maintaining military postures consistent with the agreement — in which the strongest motivations should be expected to impel countries voluntarily to demonstrate compliance as fully as they can.

A host country may find ways of providing direct information about where its forces are, what their status is, and what they are doing, and thereby reduce the need for the examiners to find out where they are not, and what they are not doing. This may especially be the case when, through inadvertence or through the ordinary faulty working of the surveillance system, there is reason to suppose that violation is suspected.

Types of Information

If the other side violates the agreement, we certainly want to know it. But we may want to know more than just *whether* a participant is cheating. We may want to know how much he is cheating, how long he has been doing it, in what ways, and how he got away with it before we caught him. If he is cheating on something like a test ban, or in the development and construction of weapons, we shall surely want the best intelligence we can get about what he has learned, what he has developed, and how much he has constructed. Again we see that the problem is not quite like that of apprehending a criminal in the cops and robbers analogy; it is a little more like our wanting to know what he has done with the stolen goods, what the techniques were by which he escaped apprehension for so long, and whether he is still running his rackets while incarcerated.

But the matter is related, too, to how well the system will deter violation. Here there are some dilemmas. On the one hand, if our surveillance is good we want him to know it so that he has the highest regard for our capability of detecting violation. At the same time, the better he knows what it is that we know, the better he is able to adapt to the weaknesses in our system.

Deterrence of Violation

Implicit in any desire to monitor compliance is the notion of deterrence. Inspection is based on the assumption that countries might violate if they could get away with it; catching them after the fact is one motive for our keeping them under surveillance, but eliminating the incentive is probably at least as important.

Detection and deterrence are related, in that the *expectation* of detection is an important deterrent. The more likely it is that the country could get away with violation, the less the violation will be deterred. Just as no system can be confidently expected to detect violation with certainty, no system can be expected to deter absolutely.

In some cases a modest capability of detection would deter any thought of violation; in other cases, depending on what the costs and gains are, a quite respectable probability of detection might not altogether deter violation. (We cannot be sure that the probability of detection the other country has in mind, when it resists or succumbs to the temptation, is the same probability that we ourselves estimate. If he exaggerates the effectiveness of our surveillance, we gain in deterrence; if he underestimates our information or alertness to the evidence or our resolve to react to his violation, he may feel freer to violate than we think he does.)

The motive to violate is bound to depend on what is gained by it. Violations that would be profitable only if violation is repeated numerous times, or continues over a long period, may be unattractive even in the face of a fairly "inefficient" detection system. The system may have repeated opportunities to detect violation. If the stationing of submarines in prohibited areas, or the construction of civil defenses, or the testing of nuclear weapons, must go on for a long period before the cumulative fruits become attractive, or before the opportunity for exploitation presents itself, a small probability of detection on each day or on each occurrence may compound into a large likelihood that the violation will be detected before it has done exorbitant harm.

The calculation also depends on whether the benefits of violation, once violation is detected, are retroactively lost. Clandestine research and development, clandestine intelligence or training activities, may be valuable for as long as they continue; all that is lost upon detection is continuation of the opportunity. But with clandestine preparations against which quick countermeasures are possible, or clandestine research that will yield technical knowledge to the other side as soon as it detects the violation, the advantages are lost altogether unless detection is avoided.

Finally, the costs and risks of detection itself may be modest or may be enormous. One of the risks is that the arms agreement is destroyed and arms control is discredited for a long time. In that case, the fruits of violation must outweigh the benefits of the arms control, when the chances of detection and denunciation are weighed in the balance. But more than that may be involved; the other country — the one whose interests have been violated — may take disproportionate action. The result may be a more furious arms race, or other political or military countermeasures, that make it an enormous net disadvantage ever to have entered into the agreement with intent to violate.

In any case, the calculation is surely complex, including not only the difficulties of organizing a violation but of keeping the benefits secret afterwards and of maintaining internal morale and cohesion. Clandestine development of a weapon may be of reduced value if the weapon itself, once produced, is bound to be seen — especially if it will be copied. Clandestine organization is the more difficult, the less a government can afford to permit internal knowledge that violation is going on. Even the Soviet government, with its talents for internal secrecy, would find it difficult to exploit secretly a violation that required its military planning be geared to the violation, or if its foreign policy and military activities required widespread internal knowledge of what was going on.

All of these factors enter a judgment of the likelihood that violation will occur and, if so, on what scale and with what success. It would be a mistake to suppose that any system will deter perfectly. But the probability of violation may be brought within tolerable bounds, or better than that, by a reasonably good system of detection if the agreement does not provide enormous irreversible gains from occasional violation. And even if violation cannot with great confidence be completely deterred, it may be sufficient to deter the most profitable violations, or to make violation so costly that little can be gained by it.

Inspection Without Arms Limitation

It was remarked above that an arms limitation could in principle omit all reference to inspection by adopting the principle that it was the responsibility of complying participants to satisfy each other in any way they could. There is also the opposite possibility; that an agreement could provide for improved surveillance and intelligence without specifying limitations on arms. The open-skies idea, which was intended to take the "surprise" out of surprise attack and so to make it unattractive, is one such example. But the possibilities go beyond that.

Much of the arms race — both in the procurement and in the development of weapons — may involve each side's "over-responding" to the other's behavior. Whatever aspect of the arms race we have in mind, it is usually some kind of reciprocated military preparation in which each side's force level or development or deployment is a response to what it perceives to be the other's forces, programs and deployments. There is an important possibility that, in the absence of reliable knowledge, each may err in imputing more strength, success, or activity to the other than is actually the case. In these circumstances, better knowledge on each side about what the other is doing might appreciably dampen the arms competition.

The opposite could be the case. If both underestimate each other, or if both rationalize their own programs as "adequate" in the absence of irrefutable evidence to the contrary, clearer indication of what each is doing might galvanize the other into greater activity, and accelerate the arms race. Nevertheless, better facilities on both sides for keeping track of each other would probably deflate some alarm based on exaggerated estimates or on an obsession with the worst possible contingency.

It is also possible that deliberate steps in the direction of more stable weapons or lower levels of weaponry, or deliberate restraint in the deployment of forces, would be reciprocated if both sides knew that their moves could be perceived and that they could tell whether or not reciprocation had occurred. If we think of arms control as including informal measures taken with a view to reciprocation, rather than explicit understandings arrived at by overt negotiation, some improvement in surveillance and intelligence may be a prerequisite to carrying this process very far.

It is therefore not illogical that inspection procedures might be explicitly provided while any limitations on arms were outside the agreement. This is admittedly a special case, but it helps to emphasize that the arms limitations and the surveillance procedures, while related, may not be closely related.

Problems in Inspection

It was mentioned that inspection could lead to an increase in tensions if it were poor at screening out false evidence of violation. The inspection itself could prove to be irritating in relations among participants, if any large scale detectivry is involved. The system, therefore, must be judged not only on whether it adequately gets at the information, but on whether it entails inconveniences or financial costs on such a scale as to be an irritation between governments or between populations and the "foreign inspectors." One reason for selecting nationalities that are less "sensitive" for the inspection job, for those kinds of inspection that do not require the utmost loyalty to the recipient of the information, is to minimize these irritants. There have been suggestions that the inspecting forces be given, where possible, positive and constructive roles to perform. Joint research programs are cited as an example.

The cost of inspection, in straightforward monetary terms, has also to be kept in mind. The personnel ought to be of the highest quality obtainable. They should be not only beyond the reach of bribery and intimidation but beyond any suspicion of it, and beyond reproach in their behavior. To reduce irritation they should be selected and trained to perform well in a mission that has an element of diplomacy. They must have a continuous sense of responsibility and urgency. And they may need a good deal of technical training, including such mundane things as languages. If high morale and low turnover require decent family arrangements, these would have to be provided and paid for. Finally, there may be some quite exotic equipment costs, if surveillance in space, at sea, in the air, and so forth is required, and if a high degree of mobility and continuous communications are required.

Finally, there is the likelihood that some inspection procedures may contravene domestic laws, rights of individuals, even constitutional privileges. While these do not appear to be insurmountable obstacles, the procedures will have to be designed to take these into account.*

Excessive Information

One of the difficulties in any inspection scheme is that it is bound to yield information beyond its intended purposes. This is partly because the personnel and techniques of surveillance will simply "see" a lot of things other than the particular objects and activities that they are intended to monitor. It is partly because some of the very knowledge required in order to verify compliance, or in order to safeguard against dangerous military preparations outside the agreement, will itself be "sensitive" information. That is, it will be information that can be misused by the inspecting country, or that is conducive to military instability. The obvious example, and one that is alleged to underlie the Soviet depreciation of inspection and control, is the acquisition of targeting information for a strategic attack as a by-product of an inspection system intended to reduce vulnerability.

The use of sampling, of unmanned detection stations, or of deliberately degraded equipment, are of interest for precisely this reason.

Sampling

Many jobs of inspection or surveillance can be simplified and reduced in scope by the use of sampling techniques. Ordinarily sampling, as compared with a complete examination of the entire population of objects to be kept under surveillance, achieves savings in cost or administrative nuisance at some expense in information. Sampling can provide a reasonable approximation at a reasonable cost, rather than complete accuracy at unreasonable cost. But in arms control there is an additional strong reason for the introduction of sampling.

The reason is that "too much" information of certain sensitive kinds may be as harmful as too little, or even more harmful. As long as any kind of military secrecy is conducive to security, observation and inspection will be tolerable only if they yield the right

* Cf. Louis Henkin, *Arms Control and Inspection in American Law.* New York: Columbia University Press, 1958.

kind of information without yielding too much of the wrong kind. But where the "wrong kind" is targeting information — information useful in an attack — it may be closely correlated with precisely the kind of information that is legitimate under the arms control.

For example, it may be difficult to examine missile sites or aircraft to see whether the agreement is complied with, without obtaining excessive or even intolerable knowledge of their precise locations. Alternatively, it may be impossible to require aircraft or submarines to assemble for inspection without so interfering with their operations, and without so increasing their vulnerability, as to make such examination intolerable.

Sampling is one way of getting around these difficulties. The essential idea of sampling is that a properly chosen sample may be so representative of the entire population of things to be examined that, within certain limits, one can suppose that what is true of the sample is true of the larger population. And in arms control, the main characteristic of a "properly chosen" sample is that the party being examined not be able to anticipate the individual objects or activities that will form the sample. Selection at random is invariably part of a good sampling process.

An important difference between ordinary statistical sampling, and the use of sampling against an intelligent adversary, is that the activities being monitored may adapt themselves to the sampling procedure that is chosen. If there is a limit, for example, on the number of samples that can be taken within a given month or a year, and the limit has been exhausted, violations may proceed with impunity until the next period begins; and if the examiner guards against this by saving part of his quota towards the end of the period, he risks wasting it. Again, if the party being examined knows what kinds of behavior will appear suspicious, he may deliberately create suspicious evidence in order to exhaust the sample. On the other hand, if the examiner is allowed a sample check on every occurrence of suspicious evidence, he may claim the right to sample so often that he achieves excessive information in spite of the sample limits. Like any other part of the enforcement scheme, the sampling procedure is subject to abuse on one side or the other.

It is important to note that for some important kinds of sampling procedures, one has to be able to identify the *individual objects* under examination. Consider the following case. Suppose there

were an understanding that all of one's aircraft, or all of one's submarines, should be within certain geographical areas, but for their
own protection they were not to be under continuous and exhaustive surveillance. If, say, a small fraction of the submarine force
could be observed each day, or even just on certain days chosen at
random, there would be an appreciable likelihood that any significant violation of the rules would be detected, and there would be
little or no chance that compliance would lead to mistaken evidence of violation. But it is certainly not sufficient just to produce
each day, for observation, a small number of submarines. The submarines that surface for observation must truly be chosen at random or chosen in some way that the submarine force itself cannot
anticipate. If each submarine has a serial number, the examiner can
choose a few numbers at random, requiring submarines with those
particular numbers to surface and demonstrate that they are within
the agreed bounds. But for this it is essential that the *individual*
submarines that surface be identified. In other words, these must
be the particular submarines that correspond to the sample chosen
by the examiner, and not simply some submarines produced by the
examinee. For some purposes, perhaps for surfaced submarines, it
may not be too difficult to effect the individual identification; in
other cases, such as patrolling aircraft, the identification of individuals may be extremely difficult.

Unilateral Intelligence

We have emphasized the relation of formal inspection to unilateral intelligence, as supplements to each other. There is another
relation that needs to be noted. It is that many techniques of surveillance, sources of information, and kinds of intelligence, that are
presently relied on could be disturbed or precluded by the institution of formal procedures.

The agreement itself and the spirit behind it may be incompatible with some techniques of intelligence. Also, it may be more difficult to deny what one is doing if both sides have better access to
each other's behavior. Furthermore, agreements on the kinds of
surveillance that each is permitted to exercise over the other may
tend to deny implicitly certain other kinds of intelligence gathering. Overflights might be an example: an agreement that permitted
specified overflights would implicitly be an agreement not to con-

duct overflights outside those bounds. An agreement on certain rights of inspection would often be an implicit denial of other rights.

The point is raised here only to indicate that the intelligence implications of arms control go beyond those that are explicitly the concern of the agreement itself, and that an inspection system can probably not be viewed as something simply superimposed on existing sources of information. This point can be viewed negatively, as suggesting that we may lose certain intelligence as we gain other; it can conceivably be looked at positively, as a regularizing of certain forms of intelligence, and possibly the elimination of some aspects of the "intelligence race" that it could be mutually beneficial to eliminate.

Chapter 10

REGULATING AN
ARMS AGREEMENT

As already stressed, the function that is usually described as "inspection" does not operate in isolation from the other techniques of observation and intelligence gathering, nor is it solely — perhaps not even mainly — oriented towards the verification of compliance with the specific limitations contained in an agreement. But even for the verification of compliance, "inspection" is much too narrow a concept. "Inspectors" and "inspectorate" suggest a police-like effort to get at the *facts*, with a view to seeing whether the enemy is willfully cheating on an agreement — it being supposed that if he is cheating he will try to hide it but that, given all the facts, one can tell whether or not cheating has occurred.

But the job is likely to entail judgment and interpretation, not just a look at the "facts." It will involve continual administration and regulation, as well as continual argument and negotiation. The "inspection" concept suggests an analogy with fraud or rum-running; but if the analogy is tax evasion, regulation of monopolies, or enforcement of international-trade agreements, "inspection" may be not only inadequate but somewhat off the central point.

Two analogies are helpful in getting perspective on the problem. One is the budget process. Ordinarily the Budget Bureau and the Department of Defense try to enforce a variety of limits, ceilings, and restraints on the military services. The services try to avoid them with all the skill and persistence they can muster, sometimes with an excess of zeal. The Budget Bureau does not "inspect" the Air Force to see whether it is "cheating" in its budget program in order to get more equipment, personnel, or operating expenses than it deserves. Rather, it "examines" the Air Force to see whether the Air Force is "justified" in its "interpretation" of the consequences of its budget program. An agency under budget examination, whether civilian or military, will depreciate the equipment that it possesses, exaggerate the obsolescence rate, discount its spare-parts inventory, exaggerate the need for a flow of parts and materials in the "pipeline," and err on the safe side in the calculation of reliability coefficients, absentee and out-of-commission rates, rejects, and the prices it will pay for materials and equipment.

Getting the *facts* is only part of the examiner's task; the harder part is arguing over the interpretations, projections, forecasts, and evaluations of significance of the facts at hand. And almost always what is the object of examination is a situation at some future point in time, so that even the pertinent "facts" are estimates and projections.

A second helpful analogy is like arms control in reverse. It is the process of holding an allied country *up* to some agreed level of armament, in contrast to keeping a potential enemy *down* to some agreed level. In NATO, and under some of the mutual security agreements between the United States and allied countries, the United States has called on other countries (and they have sometimes called on the United States) to meet particular arms goals. In NATO there have been agreements among the participating countries about the forces that the individual countries were "committed" to make available. Similarly, countries have had to justify their requests for military assistance by indicating the forces that were ready, or would be ready on schedule, to utilize the equipment and supplies that were programmed.

Here the problem is to prove not that one's forces are lower than some ceiling, but that they are up to some agreed floor. Experience suggests that in arguing whether a country has or has not met its commitment to put a certain number of "combat-ready" divisions in the field, or to have some number of aircraft "operational," the problems have less to do with the detection of willful fraud than with evaluations, interpretations, and forecasts. Whether French forces in North Africa are "available" to NATO; whether a particular German armored division is 75 per cent combat ready; whether a British aircraft-production program is consistent with a programmed number of squadrons operational by a particular date, are not so much questions of fact as of forecast, interpretation, and evaluation. It is obvious that even men of good will, well informed and even equally informed, can differ over these interpretations.

An Illustrative Arms Limitation

The problem can be illustrated by a particular, and rather arbitrary, weapon limitation. Consider an agreement limiting the number of "missiles" on each side to 100. (The number is arbitrary, and the reader can think of 10 or 1,000 if he wishes.) This particular limitation is almost unique in its simplicity: "A missile is a missile" is probably closer to being true and precise than is "A division is a division," "A squadron is a squadron," "A ship is a ship," or "An officer is an officer." If we expressed the limit not in terms simply of the number of missiles but of the military capabilities of the missiles, we should have to deal with payload, warhead yield, range, reliability, state of readiness, vulnerability under attack, and other discounts and coefficients of effectiveness. In other words, 100 missiles seems reasonably clear cut. (Many of the difficulties to be mentioned would disappear if the limit were put at zero; on the other hand, not nearly all of them would.)

But what is a 100–missile limit? Does it refer to the average number of missiles available in the course of a year, or in the course of a month, or at any given moment? If one side goes over the limit momentarily, even inadvertently, does it go under for a while to compensate; does it pay a penalty; does it permit the other side a similar excess for a similar period; or is it accused of cheating and denounced? If one side has exceptional success in the production of replacements, and ends up with more ready missiles than it expected and runs over the ceiling, must it destroy them or can it impound them and use them for replacement at a later date? And if one is allowed to compensate overage with some underage, working towards an average of 100 missiles, how does the other tell whether the first is abusing the scheme by developing excessive peaks justified by previous troughs?

What about spare parts? Spare parts are relevant both to the maintenance of the missiles, i.e., to the question of what average fraction of the 100 are in the state of readiness, and to the possibility of constructing additional missiles in an emergency. The strategic significance of 100 missiles depends on how many could be fired at once on short notice, how many could be fired within an hour, within four hours, within a day, within a week, and so forth. The schedule relating missiles ready to the elapsed time from some decision to fire may depend on the spare-parts allowance.

Something similar is true of components in the production process. As long as there is current production of missiles there is going to be inventory, and goods in transit, all the way from the launching pads back to the assembly lines, from the assembly lines back to the producers of components, and so on back to the raw materials.

There is also a problem of weapons out of commission. A squadron of missiles may be assigned 10 weapons with launching facilities for 9; on the average it may take 10 weapons available to keep 9 in condition to be fired. The tenth is a "spare" to replace whichever one of the nine is momentarily out of condition. If the agreement is based on a number that is presumed ready to fire on short notice, one has to multiply the basic number by some factor (like our 10/9) to determine what gross number of missiles is required to provide a force that is up to the limit. But this itself requires defining "readiness" under a variety of conditions. These conditions involve the minutes, hours, or days of delay that would be allowed in the standard definition, as well as how much advance notice of a decision to fire is assumed. The conditions must also allow for climate, season, quality of the crew, base configuration, dispersal, and mode of operation or time-on-station of any mobile missiles. And there can be no general expectation that these conditions would be identical for all countries.

Then there is the "pipeline." If there is going to be replacement of missiles there will be missiles in process of assembly, undergoing test or examination, en route to launching stations, and so forth. The replacement rate would be a critical factor. Missiles are replaced both to improve them and because they may suffer damage and aging, as well as because they may be consumed in occasional testing. If missiles are replaced at the rate of 10 per cent per year, the corresponding productive capacity would be low in relation to the finished inventory, and one would have to run his assembly lines for some years at the normal replacement rate to make an appreciable addition to the finished inventory. If instead one replaces missiles at the rate of 10 per cent per month, the finished inventory could be doubled in a year's time by using current production for additions to stock rather than for substitution. So the significance of current productive capacity, if the latter is geared to the replacement rate, depends on the replacement rate allowed. Something similar is true for testing. Test missiles not only represent missiles that must be either included or excluded in the count, but they also represent production and productive capacity in addition to the "normal" productive capacity required for replacement and improvement.

Finally, there are the "exchange rates" among missiles. "One hundred missiles" says nothing about size. We could say that a missile is a missile, whether it carries 500, 5,000 or 50,000 pounds of payload; whether it has a single warhead or multiple warheads; whether it is dispersed as an individual target, clustered with other missiles in a silo, or is shipmate to a dozen other missiles on a submarine. Just as missiles may differ from each other in their penetration and payload capability, they can differ from each other in their target significance; three missiles in a silo may be like one missile in their vulnerability. If a particular type of missile is not uniformly specified in an agreement, there will arise a need to make quantitative comparisons among the different kinds of weapons, with discounts, exchange rates, or other corrections to be applied to the gross number depending on the character of the missile.

The problem can of course be simplified by ignoring these differences. But it would not necessarily be wise to simplify it in that way. Except for the convenience of simplicity — a convenience that certainly deserves to be emphasized — there may be no logical reason to suppose that individual enumeration of missiles is the best way of measuring the military significance of a strategic force.

Failure to discriminate among types of missiles could mean that each side was simply forced into the largest missiles available, when it might have been willing to have a lesser force — as measured in yield or payload — if it could have had a somewhat larger number of smaller missiles. One might measure the force not in missiles, but say, deliverable megatonnage. This, too, is a very crude index of strategic-force effectiveness, and could lead to peculiar distortions in, say, the size and number of missiles. To take another example, a limitation on the total number of submarine-based missiles, that paid no attention to the way missiles are clustered on a submarine, might just lead to the dispersion of missiles among a larger number of smaller submarines, in the interest of greater versatility and lesser vulnerability. This might not be a bad thing, but it also might be wasteful. And it must be kept in mind that limitations that appear "unreasonable" to the military services are not likely to enjoy the respect of the military services.

Many of these problems are aggravated if the agreement itself is not perfectly symmetrical between the two sides. The definitions of the discounts, the coefficients of effectiveness, as well as the techniques and procedures for inspection, would be quite different for a force of submarine-based missiles and a force of fixed land-based missiles, different again from rail-mobile or airborne missiles. If for reasons of cost, technology, geography, tradition, or sheer preference, we and the Russians develop qualitatively different missile forces, the inspection problems will be very different on both sides; and on questions like those raised above, the problem is not simply to arrive at answers that both sides can agree to, but to arrive at *dissimilar* answers for the two sides that nevertheless make sense in relation to the weapon systems on the two sides and that are in some sense "equivalent." (It should be noticed that we have further simplified our hypothetical problem by supposing that there are only two sides, and that the numbers allowed on both sides are equivalent.)

What has been said about missiles, spare parts, replacement rates, and so on, can also be said about launching sites, crews, etc. If it is easier to hide missiles than to hide trained crews, or at least easier to keep hidden missiles in good condition than to keep hidden crews in good condition, a nation that wishes either to violate the agreement or to be prepared for a breakdown of the agreement may wish to keep an excess of crews relative to the permitted number of missiles. But what is an excess number of crews? This will depend on whether crews work in four-hour or eight-hour shifts, whether they rotate among jobs and sites, on the ratio of time on duty to time off duty, on the allowance for sickness and absenteeism, on the base configuration, the dispersal of missiles, and so forth. (The more dispersed the crews, the greater will be the spare-personnel requirements, as well as the spare-parts requirements.)

The "supply" of crews will also depend on the reserve status of crews that are out of service, on the enlistment period, and so forth. This would be especially true if one were concerned not so much with what the enemy could do on a moment's notice if he launched a surprise attack after cheating, but with who is ahead in case the arms race is resumed. Trained crews, if they involve long lead time, may be as important as missile-production capacity in the event of a sudden resumption of the arms race. The question of which side is in a better position three, six, or twelve months after the agreement breaks down may depend on which side has not only expansible productive capacity but trained crews in reserve. Here again we are dealing with a matter of judgment, both on the strategic significance of trained crews in existence and on the justifiability of the particular table of organization, manning doctrine, or military-personnel policy.

To the above problems must be added all those connected with the "phasing in" of new missiles. It is hard to imagine limitations so tight that all technological improvement would be ruled out; certainly defects in design, potential improvements in reliability, improvements in command and control, in reduction of accidents, and so forth, suggest that superior missiles would be replacing earlier models and that replacement rates would be affected by the urge to improve one's weapons. It has to be stressed that not all such "improvements" are in contradiction of the spirit of the agreement. But this phasing of new missiles further complicates the issues raised above about productive capacity, pipeline, replacement rate, testing, spare parts, and crew training.

Interpretation of the Agreement

The above remarks are intended to suggest that, however clear and precise the notion of "100 missiles" may appear to be, the detailed implications of such a limitation are complicated. This means that either the agreement itself must be extraordinarily detailed in covering all the parameters suggested by the questions raised above, or the agreement must be taken as giving just a few bench marks from which all the ramifications are to be derived by negotiation, analysis, argument, adjustment, and trial and error. One can suppose an agreement that is *expressed* in terms of the finished inventory of ready missiles, but that is intended to imply that all ancillary activities and inventories are to be scaled in appropriate proportion to this one bench mark, to the number of ready missiles allowed to be on hand. An agreement that covered all of these ancillary points in detail would be at best a serious nuisance, unless it were subject to easy and continual changes; so on either interpretation it seems evident that there would need to be a continual process of judgment, accommodation, negotiation, evaluation, and adaptation.

It might be supposed that an agreement on a single bench mark, if properly understood by both sides with a will to make it work, necessarily implies a sufficient understanding on these ancillary questions to make it fairly easy to judge whether, in subsequent examination and negotiation, the participants are behaving in reasonable accord with the intent of the agreement. But this could be a wrong supposition. It may be hard enough to reach agreement on weapon limitations themselves. To suppose that agreement is reached on the *intent* of the agreement, on every aspect of its interpretation, on the motives behind it, on the context it fits into, and on what it is supposed to lead to, is to ask more of a sensitive agreement between potential enemies than one asks for in an alliance between friendly nations or even in an ordinary piece of domestic legislation.

What makes statutory law possible in democratic society, and what may make arms-control agreements possible, is that people and nations can agree on actions, restraints, laws, and programs, without necessarily agreeing in detail on their purpose or on the expected state of the world at every future point in time. (To reach such detailed agreement might take more time than would be wise to take in arriving at an agreement.) And a limitation on the number of missiles could have several quite different alternative purposes, including purposes that have never been the subject of articulate agreement even within a government, to say nothing of agreement between governments.

One interpretation of such a limitation is simply that 100 (or whatever the agreed number is) is the proper number, in the sense that more would be too dangerous in the case of war, fewer would be inadequate for deterrence. Another interpretation is that 100 missiles is right for the time being but that it is a step on the way to zero, and that a nation that has reached agreement on the numerical limit has implicitly agreed in spirit to reduce that number by agreement as soon as possible. Under this general interpretation, questions of detail would presumably be decided on the stingy side in order to promote the downtrend.

A third interpretation is that the correct number of missiles to have on hand is zero but neither side wants to be completely without productive capacity in the event the agreement breaks down. Therefore each side is to be allowed, in principle, a "proper" level of productive capacity, with some minimum number of missiles to keep the crews trained, to permit test programs, to experiment with base configurations, and so forth. In other words, the whole force is a "stand-by" force, not in stand-by for the event of war but for the event of rearmament. The 100 missiles are a "cadre" to make expansion possible; and the stipulation of 100 missiles is simply a shorthand way of stipulating an appropriate level of production facilities, crews, training facilities, test facilities, research and development, and so forth. It is a bench mark to suggest the general level of activity. The number of finished missiles, in this interpretation, is just a convenient bottleneck for specifying a general scale of strategic-force activity.

A fourth interpretation is that both sides hope, by reciprocal unilateral action, to reduce substantially all of their strategic forces, but have not yet been able to agree on limits on aircraft, surface ships, etc. The limitation to 100 missiles is an agreed first step, and its main purpose is to symbolize what in principle has been agreed with respect to the rest of the strategic force. In that case this particular limitation is essentially an experiment, a symbolic gesture, a practice run, a test of each other's intentions; and the purpose of inspection, examination, and so forth, is not so much to see whether the particular 100–missile limitation is being met but whether the entire national strategic posture is consistent with the attitude symbolized by this particular limitation.

And there must be other interpretations. Not only may interpretations differ on both sides, but there may be different understandings and interpretations within the government of a participating nation, or among allied countries that reach an agreed negotiating position. Thus there may be genuine substantive differences among the participants to an agreement in the interpretation of intent and performance under the agreement, and in the settlement of the disputes that arise.

Implications for Inspection

If this view is correct, it follows that the range of activities in each country that is properly subject to examination or surveillance may go well beyond the particular inventory or activity stipulated in the agreement itself. If, for example, the agreement is reasonably easy to monitor in terms of the inventory of finished missiles, or at least if the excess number that could be obtained by padding the force or by clandestine evasion would not be strategically significant, one is likely to be mainly concerned with the productive capacity for rearmament that the other country has. Productive capacity is relevant to what happens if the agreement breaks down. Each side wants to be reasonably sure that the other is not in a dangerously advantageous position to resume the arms race.

Productive capacity has many dimensions, including the time dimension. For some purposes, productive capacity can be described in terms of the size of the missile force that can be achieved by different dates, starting from some moment when the agreement is broken. One wants to know where the other side would be in thirty days, ninety days, one year, or three years, if the arms race were to resume. For the short period it is the inventory plus the pipeline and the components; for an intermediate period it is goods-in-process; for a somewhat longer period it is production and assembling capacity; for an even longer period it may be research and development. In all cases the analysis must include launching facilities, crews, communications, defenses, and any other vehicles required, as well as the various resources that go into the missiles themselves.

This does not mean that each side needs highly detailed and absolutely reliable estimates of everything concerned with rearmament production. It does mean that each side has to be in possession of sufficient facts and estimates to be reasonably assured that there is little likelihood that it has been dangerously disadvantaged. In any event, this argument suggests that the scope of the examination or surveillance should in principle be broad.

Looking at the agreement in this way gives us another interpretation of the missile limitation itself. One could view it as essentially a "strategic-warning system." A limitation on the number of finished missiles, if it can be adhered to, essentially means that neither side can attack the other with any appreciable success until some period of time after it has broken the agreement. The length of time required to build up a dominant force then depends on productive capacity, bottlenecks, and so forth. The breakdown of the agreement is the "warning" that each side requires in order to step up its own production.

In this interpretation, one views the agreement not in terms of the significance of the 100 missiles on each side, but on the warning he would get and the time he would have to respond if the other side broke away from the agreement. If, starting from an inventory not greatly different from the 100 missiles specified in the agreement, and from productive facilities roughly commensurate with that level, it would take the other side X months to speed up production and produce enough missiles to attack one's own force with any great success, one can expect something like X months' warning in which to increase (or to defend better) his own strategic force, or to take appropriate military and diplomatic countermeasures.

It is also apparent that each side must continually appraise the other side's intentions. How to interpret an apparent bulge in the other side's missile force or productive facilities, and how to interpret evidence that the other side is engaged in research and development designed to shorten the lead time in the event the arms race is resumed, depends on what evidence there is about the other side's intentions and capabilities. If it appears that the other side would be able, in a crash program, to double the number of his missiles within a few weeks by hastening assembly, by utilizing spare components, by speeding deliveries, and by intensified maintenance of the missiles that he has, this may be dangerous or not — strategically significant or not — according as he is or is not taking other action consistent with intentions to launch an attack within some comparable period of time. The more one can examine the context within which resumed armament might take place — such context including air defenses, civil defenses, the movement and deployment of aircraft, and so forth — the better one can evaluate the significance of particular abnormalities in behavior that may be observed.

The Regulatory Process

The sample of problems raised above is not intended to be complete but to illustrate that "inspection" is only part of the problem, and "facts" are not enough. The question is not simply the one of cheating or playing fair. The process may be more like a regulatory function than like a criminal procedure. True, there can be willful cheating on a large scale of a sort that, if one can find evidence, one can recognize as willful cheating on a large scale. But there may also be enormous room for differences of opinion about evaluation and interpretation of a country's military activities. What looks like cheating may be the equivalent of budget padding. Even willful cheating, such as one may find in the echelons of a government agency during a budget hearing, may not have been commanded or even hoped for by the higher echelons. Government agencies, including military services, often circulate instructions to subordinates engaged in budget planning to the effect that they are to develop scrupulously honest estimates, to avoid padding, both for the sake of economy and for the sake of developing a clean record with the examining agency. Yet the subordinates who do the budget planning may nevertheless violate the instructions out of a sense of bureaucratic zeal and responsibility, or may discount the instructions as window dressing, or may anticipate that the examiners will never believe that the padding has been eliminated and will cut to compensate for the invisible padding, and so pad accordingly. It can be difficult for the top level of an agency to keep lower levels from overestimating requirements, underestimating inventory, and depreciating assets. In any case, the matter is one of evaluation and interpretation, projection and forecast, almost never one of "facts" alone.

If this is an important part of the problem, there are implications for the kind of examiners or enforcement bodies, for the talents required, for the relation to the host country, for the techniques of surveillance and interrogation, for the relation to clandestine and other unilateral intelligence, and even for the public relations of their role and the question of their nationality and loyalty. There are implications for what happens when one detects an evasion, or suspects one, or finds something untoward.

In the usual analogy of the detective vs. the criminal, one gathers his evidence and springs it on the subject with all the implications of guilt. But there is a difference between willful breaking of the law and normal bending of the rules, between tight conspiracy and disorganized bureaucracy. In the one case you indict your enemy; in the other you argue with him. In the one case he either is guilty or is not (whether or not you can prove it); in the other case it is a matter of judgment, with room for genuine differences of opinion, and with a possible gamut of motives between the extremes of willful, conspiratorial, hierarchical cheating on the one hand, and innocently disorganized stretching of the rules on the other. Even criminal cases have that nice simplicity only in paperback fiction.

Chapter 11

THE ARMS BUDGET
AND THE ECONOMY

Discussion of arms control and the American economy is usually a blend of two ingredients — welcome relief at all the money to be saved, and anxiety about whether the economy can take it. Lower taxes, better schools, more housing, and campaigns against disease are widely proposed as ways of either fore-, stalling depression or enjoying our savings. Massive programs of foreign assistance have been proposed and, at times, implicitly promised. But however we weigh the opportunities and dangers in a sizable reduction of the more than forty billion dollars that we now spend on defense, we have first to ask whether arms control would bring such a reduction.

And it is by no means obvious that arms control, even rather comprehensive arms control, would entail rapid and substantial reductions in military outlays. Aside from the costs associated with the inspection and regulation of military activities — which might be appreciable — there is the more important consideration that many forms of arms control would not necessarily reduce the cost of military programs. It is quite possible that arms control would increase them.

Limited-War Forces

A few examples will emphasize the point. Suppose arrangements are devised, or understandings reached, that have the purpose — or at least the effect — of inhibiting the introduction of nuclear weapons into limited war. One consequence may be an increased

120

outlay on military forces equipped with more conventional fire-power; and this would not necessarily be a violation of the spirit of the arms control. In fact, if we keep in mind that many of the advocates of nuclear weapons for limited war have emphasized the economy involved in these weapons, it does not seem unnatural that to avoid reliance on nuclear weapons we may sacrifice some expected "savings."

Or consider measures that succeed in reducing the advantage, in the event of general war, of initiating it, and that succeed in allaying the fear of surprise attack. As argued earlier, the danger of accidental war as well as of premeditated war might thereby be substantially reduced. So might the danger of "escalation" of small wars into a general war, and the danger of local military crises erupting into a general war through each side's obsession with the importance of striking first. One of the consequences of the success of such arrangements is that the world may be made safer for smaller wars and other forms of violence, provocation, and harassment. A natural consequence might well be increased outlays on the kinds of military force required in a world in which the threat of massive retaliation, or the threat of accidental enlargement of a conflict, has lost much of its power to inhibit small-scale aggression.

Here again it helps to keep in mind that reliance on the threat of general war as a means of policing the world against limited aggression has been at least partly motivated by economy. Measures that successfully reduce these threats on both sides might well be expected to eliminate some of those economies.

Second-Strike Forces

Again, consider the effect of an understanding that both sides will exert themselves to develop strategic forces that are as nearly invulnerable as possible, with reliable and invulnerable communications, command, and control arrangements, and with safeguards against false alarms or unauthorized actions; and to pursue modes of deployment that minimize the danger of misinterpretation and misunderstanding. If successful, such measures deserve to be considered a very important kind of arms control. But even aside from the possible implications for limited war, the costs of pursuing these objectives might raise defense budgets.

"Invulnerable" strategic forces consist not only of weapons and

vehicles but of communications, command and control arrangements, warning systems, reconnaissance and intelligence, and all
the other components of the "system." Comparing, say, ballistic-
missile submarines with unprotected, fixed-base missiles of known
location, the former appear to be more consistent with the kind of
understanding just mentioned. The former are also likely to be
more expensive.

Expense in this case is tricky to define. An unprotected ICBM,
especially if eight or nine out of ten can be kept in readiness, is a
cheaper way of delivering explosive power on enemy territory if
nothing intervenes to hinder its arrival. The submarine, with
smaller missiles and appreciably less than 100 per cent time-on-
station, is more expensive. But if we compare instead the cost per
ton of explosive power delivered in unfavorable circumstances —
in the event of a war that the enemy starts — the advantage may lie
with the submarine.

The submarine has what economists call a "comparative advantage" for the retaliatory strike; a "soft" ICBM has a comparative
advantage in an initial strike. For a *given* level of retaliatory capability the submarine force provides less of a first-strike capability
than the soft ICBM; for a *given* level of first-strike capability, the
soft ICBM provides less retaliatory capability than the submarine.

That the submarine is in some respects an expensive weapon
does not necessarily imply that defense budgets go up as we move
in the direction of more "stable" strategic forces. (Nor is the submarine necessarily typical of other weapons — mobile, hardened,
airborne, or otherwise made more secure — that would enjoy similar invulnerability.) But at least this consideration provides no
clear reason to suppose that an arms understanding with the Soviets
along the lines mentioned would bring budgets down. They could
well go up. They might especially go up if we moved urgently in
the direction of these better controlled, less vulnerable weapons.
In the short run, shifts in the character of our forces could cause
appreciable budget increases.

Traffic Rules

Consider now some other understandings we might reach, "traffic rules" for example. It is sometimes argued that airborne alert for
the bomber force is a "stabilizing" measure; it provides assurance

that we *could* retaliate after an attack, therefore greater assurance that the Soviets *would* not attack, and we need then be less hasty in a crisis. At the same time, it has been argued that airborne alert is "provocative" in getting a fraction of our bomber force in a state of alert that could be exploited for a quick effort to knock out Soviet bombers and missiles. Airborne alert has also been considered more conducive to false alarms, ambiguous accidents, or faulty communications and the danger of erroneous decisions.

Suppose it were concluded that there is truth on both sides. A possibility is to redesign airborne alert to preserve the advantage of mobile bombers while minimizing their apparent menace, reducing the likelihood of enemy misinterpretation, and improving our communications and control. In return for equivalent Soviet concessions, we might arrange flight patterns nearer to the continental United States, sacrificing proximity to target for other advantages.

This might come at a cost. There is the one-time cost of redesigning a complicated operation, testing it, moving personnel, and so forth. There might be a rise in the cost of keeping effective bombers airborne (due, for example, to the increased refueling requirements for completing potential missions from starting points farther from targets); there might be cost reductions in abandoning certain criteria of readiness, pertinent to a first-strike capability, that are expensive to maintain. But the cost implications are not obvious *a priori*.

Similar restrictions might be considered for submarines. At present our ballistic-missile submarines (and undoubtedly any Soviet missile submarines) are severely limited by the range of their missiles. To participate in a sudden well-coordinated surprise attack the boats would have to be close to the enemy. To threaten post-attack retaliation, it is somewhat less necessary to be in a state of instant readiness to launch. Depending on how much delay in response is considered consistent with deterrence, there might be a difference of several hundred miles in the proximity zones required for a first strike and for a persuasive retaliatory potential. Without discriminating against ballistic-missile submarines, we and the Russians might reach an understanding about their proximity to each other's shores. A submarine close up would be considered in position to attack; a submarine farther offshore would be in retaliatory stand-by.

Such restrictions might or might not raise costs. They might lower them. But again the point is that this kind of arms control does not obviously entail sizable reductions in the budget. It is a matter of technical examination whether costs go up or down; and to a first approximation they might not be substantially affected.

Qualitative Improvements

As in any business, accidents and unauthorized actions can be reduced by the expenditure of money. Reliability can be better achieved by spending more money. Restraints can be accommodated, and particular kinds of reduced capabilities accepted, if compensating expenditures in other directions can be made. There is in fact little presumption that the kinds of military forces that we and the Soviets might try to encourage on both sides, through our explicit and implicit arms understandings, would be of cheaper rather than more expensive quality. Even sizable quantitative reductions in strategic forces might not drastically reduce the total cost.

It has to be kept in mind that budgets are already limited by economic considerations. Measures that reduce costs and relieve budgetary strains will automatically ease the ability of governments to undertake desired expenditures for which room had not previously been found in the budgets. It should be emphasized that such offsetting expenditures do not necessarily contradict the validity or the purposes of the arms controls. Surely the effort to obtain higher quality and better trained military personnel, more reliable operating procedures, improved communications, and more safeguards against accidents, have a claim to legitimacy even in an atmosphere of arms control.

Arms Control and Military Costs

There is a sense in which arms control can be thought of as "saving money." It is this. Many of the immediate security ends that arms control might serve could to greater or lesser extent be accomplished through unilateral actions. Measures to improve intelligence and warning, to reduce false alarms and accidents, to improve discipline, to make command and communication arrangements more secure or strategic forces more secure, or to slow the tempo of decisions, can be taken unilaterally; and they almost certainly cost money. In a sense, the advantages of cooperative measures undertaken with potential enemies is that they may be more effective in achieving some of these security objectives. So one can think of arms control as a way of increasing certain kinds of military effectiveness, namely those kinds that it may be in the joint interest to increase. At the same time, arms control is aimed at *reducing* certain kinds of military capabilities, and in that sense is aimed at making it more expensive — if possible, prohibitively expensive — to achieve those kinds of military capabilities that would enhance the fear and likelihood of attack.

Adaptation to Budget Reductions

The foregoing remarks were intended to caution against expecting either the troubles or the benefits that one would expect to be associated with a substantial reduction in the federal budget. But we must consider, too, the possibility that disarmament will proceed far enough to outweigh the foregoing considerations and to make some of them irrelevant, so that the national defense budget does in fact eventually fall to a small fraction of its earlier level. What are the consequences in this case?

The point most deserving of emphasis is that the process will probably not be sudden — at least not if the disarmament is achieved through ordinary negotiation and not as a result of a crisis or war itself. A reduction of the federal budget by some tens of billions of dollars from one year to the next would of course be an enormous perturbation for the economy. The same reduction spread over four or eight years, especially if the process were anticipated, would be an event of a different order.

In either case, the economic problems can be grouped into three main classes.

First is the problem of maintaining a prosperous economy, avoiding recession or severe depression. This is essentially a matter of seeing that the aggregate demand for current output in the economy as a whole — the aggregate level of expenditure for the national product — is not reduced with the decline in the defense budget. The main offsetting components would be: (1) consumer expenditure, which would certainly respond to the sizable tax reductions that could correspond to the reduced defense outlays; (2) increased government outlays at the federal, state, and local levels,

on programs that are presently curtailed by the budgetary strain
that defense programs already impose; and (3) an increased rate
of investment in plant and equipment, highways and buildings,
residential housing, and so forth, by private businesses and individuals. The latter could be facilitated by a monetary policy adapted
to the reduced federal budget, as well as by direct federal loan
programs such as are already involved in the fields of housing and
highways, or by federal grants to local authorities.

The most desirable mix of these offsetting expenditures, and the
appropriate set of tax, monetary, and other policies to bring them
about, need not be settled or even suggested in a book on arms control. But it seems beyond doubt that adequate policies could be
devised, and that on balance the nation should be better off for being able to spend substantially less of its current income on national
defense needs and more on its productive assets and levels of current consumption.

The second main problem area is that of the "readjustment period." Assuming that reasonably full employment is maintained
through and after the transition, there will nevertheless be a substantial shift in production out of defense goods and into other
goods, and a substantial shift of personnel out of military and related services and into the civilian economy. Shifts of this kind occur continually; but the magnitude involved in a twenty to forty
billion dollar reduction in defense outlays would be substantial. It
would be about as great as the shift that occurred during the early
1950's, when resources were drawn into defense programs. It would
be a great deal less than the shift that occurred after V–J day when
the economy shifted within the space of two years from a level of
defense outlay enormously greater than our present one to a level
about half the present one. There is no strong reason to suppose that
the shock of transition under a program of gradual or even fairly
rapid disarmament would be a serious threat to the American economy. This is not to say that real difficulties would not occur, requiring careful analysis and timely measures.

The third range of problems is more difficult to characterize. It
involves the fact that a large part of technological development,
scientific research, and education within the United States is fi-
nanced by or stimulated by defense programs. Many far-reaching
technological advancements are by-products of military programs.

Not all of the resources devoted to defense efforts are a net loss to the rest of the economy. If this fact is ignored, and if the reduced requirements for defense should lead to the greater absorption of economic resources into current consumption, housing, and ordinary investment, an important component in our long-run economic growth may have been lost. It is hard to imagine that this component depends on a national-defense motivation; but unless we keep this component in mind, and make sure that comparable inducements to research and development are provided for in the period of lesser defense outlays, we shall have suffered an adverse impact of disarmament through negligence.

There are many of these intangible relations between present defense programs and the rest of the economy. Some are certainly hindrances and nuisances, some certainly valuable stimuli. These have not received the systematic study that they deserve. It would be a real challenge to our national ingenuity to see that, relieved of the necessity to spend large amounts of our national product on defense needs, we could provide even greater, rather than diminished, incentives to technological improvement, superior education and research, and economic growth.

Chapter 12

THE COLD WAR
ENVIRONMENT

THERE is no reason to suppose that an arms agreement would by itself introduce a wholly new era of international tranquility, particularly since we and the Soviet Union do not jointly control all the sources of tension and conflict in the world.

Crises and Limited War

In considering the ups and downs which an arms agreement might have to survive we must include the possibility of acute military crisis and limited war. Even a limited war between East and West, perhaps involving the military forces of some of the great powers, would not necessarily destroy the importance and value or even the fundamental basis of certain kinds of arms understandings. In fact, some arms arrangements might be deliberately designed to help cope with the danger of war or its enlargement. But the design of the arrangement, at least of the more formal arrangements involving institutions, exchange of personnel, or the granting of rights and privileges to each other, will need to take these shocks and perturbations into account.

There are a few obvious instances. Inspection and control, for example, might be substantially disturbed or circumscribed in the event of heightened military activity; it is worth while giving some thought to the status of Soviet or other foreign inspectors at Far Eastern or European air and missile bases in the event, say, of a crisis in the Taiwan Straits or of limited military activity in the area of Berlin. The same might be true with respect to inspection of, or

128

limitations on, the deployment of naval vessels in the event of their involvement in overseas military preparations or hostility.

There are also implications for the institutional arrangements, even the nationality of the personnel, for monitoring arms agreements. It might be appreciably easier to tolerate foreign inspectors at a time of crisis if they were not representatives of the nations to which we were currently most sensitive. Some of the experience of the United Nations in coping with trouble spots is pertinent here.

We must also consider that crises and limited wars could provide a cover, even a deliberately contrived cover, for evasion of the agreement; this could be true of small countries as well as large. This observation is intended not only as a warning against certain modes of evasion, but as a reminder that the motivation to intensify inspection and control might coincide with precisely those periods in which heightened inspection and control could least easily be accommodated.

There is also the possibility that crises and limited wars would be occasions for abuse of inspection and control, as well as for evasion. Exorbitant and unforeseen demands — or at least demands that seem exorbitant and unprecedented — for intensified inspection and control during such crises should be anticipated.

As remarked earlier, the difficulties of surviving such a crisis without severe damage to the arms control itself, or its discontinuance, are of strategic significance. They may help to deter aggravation of such a crisis, if some or all of the participants value the arms understanding that has been reached and restrain themselves to preserve it. By the same token, one has to contemplate that among the implied and explicit threats that would be exchanged in such a crisis would be reminders that the arms arrangements are themselves vulnerable to tensions, crises, and hostilities.

These comments relate mainly to the more formal and institutionalized kinds of arms controls. Understandings that are reached about the appropriateness of particular weapons, nationalities, or other limits to be expected in a limited war would depend more on *expectations* about each other's conduct than on formal institutions and activities. In many cases they will have been designed with precisely such a crisis in mind. On the other hand it has to be recognized that, however much both sides cooperate in creating precedents, traditions, and expectations that will inhibit the escalation of war, once a crisis is on, the motivations may be substantially changed. The purpose of such inhibitions in the first place is to make it more difficult for both sides to abandon the restraints and conventions in spite of unilateral motives for advantage that may arise in such a crisis.

It should also be kept in mind that at the height of a crisis, when both sides may perceive themselves near the brink of war, the motives in favor of arms control may become more intense. Obstacles and difficulties that were formerly insurmountable may loom less large as the urgency of arms restraint increases. One may therefore wish to anticipate that such a crisis is precisely the time when "crash disarmament" may become attractive to both sides. Alertness to the contingency may be important. Equally important may be an ability to improvise arms control under the circumstances, particularly by taking advantage of such inspection facilities as already exist as a result of more limited measures earlier agreed on.

In fact, an important reason for getting on with at least limited arrangements for inspection and control may be to have some base on which to mobilize, and from which to improvise, more urgent and important kinds of inspection and control when time does not permit analysis, negotiation, and transportation of persons and equipment on the leisurely time schedule of the cold war.

Abuse

Arms agreements, like any other agreements or institutional arrangements, can be exploited by one or more participants for purposes outside the agreement or contradictory to it. The most obvious abuse would be entering into an agreement as a means of enticing other participants to reduce their guard, in order to take direct military advantage of them. This might involve violation of the agreement itself, entering into the agreement with intent to denounce it at an opportune moment, or just using the agreement to get the enemy off guard.

But there are many other forms in which an arms agreement might be abused, though some would involve difficult judgments of intent. The Soviets have already accused the American government of seeking a nuclear-test ban, or measures to safeguard against surprise attack, for the purpose of gaining an illegitimate intelligence advantage. An arms agreement could also be used — and even the *expectation* of an arms agreement could be used — to weaken military alliances, to corrode national defense programs, and even to cause areas like West Berlin to suffer political collapse as a result of an increased expectation of eventual absorption by a neighboring or a surrounding power.

An agreement that provides for some kind of extraordinary investigation in case of suspicious evidence, such as would be involved with a nuclear-test ban but perhaps to a greater extent in connection with systems of warning against surprise attack, could be abused through frequent pretenses of suspicion and demands for invocation of the extraordinary investigating procedures. If extraordinary surveillance procedures could be invoked in a crisis, one could create a crisis or claim that a crisis was on, in order to invoke the special surveillance.

Furthermore, to the extent that successful measures of arms control reduce the danger of accidental war, one may feel free to engage in more provocative acts, including the creation of false alarms, protected by the greater security that the arms control provides, perhaps even deliberately testing the other side's military reaction to various kinds of alarms and provocations.

And there are the usual possibilities, inherent in any program in which trust and mutual confidence are incomplete, of efforts to discredit each other by claims of violation, of bad faith, of intent to denounce the agreement, and so forth.

Not all such activities would deserve to be called abuses. An effort to create a widespread expectation of disarmament, as a means of weakening military alliances and military programs, is presumably an ordinary piece of cold-war diplomacy and could be considered an "abuse" only if one took arms control to be synonymous with the elimination of international conflicts and the inauguration of a new set of rules of international behavior. Presumably, too, a minority in a democratic country could have opposed the arms control all along, and could continue to oppose it, in the sense of proposing to take advantage of any procedures for terminating the agreement. Such disagreement would presumably be "legitimate."

But any agreement is bound to have loopholes, and the loopholes may tend to discriminate in favor of one side or the other. Whether or not exploiting the loopholes is an abuse of the system is bound to be a matter of judgment, and may become a matter of subsequent negotiation. What has to be recognized is that "abuse" will usually be a matter of intent, rather than simply a matter of actions; suspicions of abuse, and accusations of abuse, must certainly be anticipated unless one expects the initiation of arms control to bring in an entirely new era in international politics.

It should not be supposed that clandestine violation is the only kind that needs to concern us. Violation may be rather open if it appears that the victim is deterred from making accusations and invoking the procedures to cope with violations. Ambiguous violation may be tolerated until it becomes traditional, so that there is no clear-cut opportunity for drawing the line and raising the issue. Open violation could even be used as an intimidation to create fear and tension, or as a means of threatening to destroy the arms control itself in the interest of coercion.

One of the difficulties with a substantial agreement on arms limitation might be the difficulty of reaching a common expectation of just how much of a "truce" in diplomacy, propaganda, and even military activity is involved. If all parties interpret the onset of an arms agreement as the turning of a new leaf in international relations, they may possibly all live up to it. If all parties expect to go on with business as usual, subject only to the particular matters agreed on, the agreement may survive. The least favorable prognosis is probably for an agreement that one party expects to symbolize the burying of the hatchet, a new era of good feeling, and a resolution to live up to new standards of international friendship, while the other takes for granted that "realistic" diplomacy will prevail, subject only to the concrete matters agreed on. In this case acute disappointment and recrimination might result, and the greatest of misunderstandings.

Disputes and Sanctions

With any arms agreement disputes will arise. Violations will be suspected and may occur. Short of open violation there may be exploitation of loopholes that contradict the spirit of the agreement, and efforts to test the bounds and limits and to get away with as much as possible.

This may occur either by deliberate government policy or by the overzealous efforts of military and civilian officials, in all the participating countries, to meet their primary responsibilities. In fact, it would not necessarily be taken for granted that to exploit loop-holes and to skirt the edge of the agreement were acts of bad faith — unless we expect all participants to take the view that the arms understandings, once reached, are outside the bounds of normal politics and to be judged by a wholly different set of standards from those that apply in agreements even among allies.

It has to be considered — and the answer is by no means obvious — whether it is wise to develop an attitude towards arms control that makes it peculiarly subject to moral judgment, tests of good faith, and a sensation that world government is in the making. Perhaps arms control should be treated as a new experiment in international relations, subject to unprecedented standards of international behavior; but it may be that to do so would be to impose a greater burden on the experiment than it could support.

Certainly the experiment would have more chance of success if the main participants had similar ideas about the rules of behavior to be expected. If both sides walk on eggs where the agreement is concerned, the agreement may survive. If both sides try to be tough, "realistic," and resilient, the agreement may be effective and durable. But if one side assumes that morality and virtue are uniquely involved in this particular international enterprise, while the other assumes that the infant must learn to survive in a world of potential conflict, tough diplomacy, and military maneuver, acute misunderstanding may result — misunderstanding that not only discredits arms control but exacerbates military and diplomatic relations.

If the agreement is accepted into the ordinary universe of international military diplomacy, we have to assume that it, like any bargain or alliance, will be an arena for international politics, will be assimilated into the threats and reassurances of the cold war, will be exploited at least by some nations for their own gain or aggrandizement, and will be the object of frequent dispute and disagreement even within countries as well as among them. Just as in the present world of moves, feints, and threats, there will be risks for those who violate as well as risks for those who charge violation. Sanctions will probably not be automatic but will depend on the willingness of certain countries to incur the risks and costs of charging violation and bringing sanctions to bear, utilizing diplomacy for the purpose. Charges of violation or bad faith will in all likelihood be handled not by solemn judicial procedures but by the usual techniques of international politics. The response to an alleged violation of the letter or the spirit of the agreement could also be subject to the kind of internal controversy that has arisen over our policy towards Quemoy, Cuba, or Berlin.

This may sound like a cynical view of arms agreements. But it is no disservice to the cause of arms control to anticipate difficulties in advance and to approach them with an attitude that tolerates some contamination of the agreement by the ordinary facts of international life.

It is sometimes thought that a nation would be so discredited by being caught in violation, or charged with violation, that all countries concerned with their image abroad would bend over backwards to keep a clean record. We can hope for this but should not count on it. Not all nations are deterred from serious military and political action by the fear that they will not seem altogether peace-loving; and not all nations would at all times rather be respected for their virtue than for their toughness. In a world that is not unanimous as to who was or is at fault in Korea, Indochina, Taiwan or Berlin, or in the Arab-Israeli dispute, it is too much to suppose that miscreants will be certain of, and certainly deterred by, a concentration of world opinion against them. In a world in which nearly unanimous opinion must have deplored the Chinese intervention in Tibet and encroachment across the Indian border, the intervention and encroachment nevertheless occurred; the deterrent effect of adverse world opinion must not be exaggerated.*

In short, arms agreements will be a part of the political-military environment. They may be a potent and mutually beneficial ingredient in that environment; but it is too much to hope that they will be immune from the cold war itself. It may be hoped, even expected, that wise and realistic arms control will allay the dangers of cold war and help to ease tensions; it is certainly too much to hope that arms control by its very inauguration will end the cold war. And to quarantine it against the facts of international political life might be to make of it an ornament and a symbol, rather than a virile restraining force.

This suggests that whatever the nominal procedure for disputes

* For an excellent discussion of the problems of applying sanctions see Fred C. Iklé, "After Detection — What?" *Foreign Affairs* XXXIX (January 1961) 208-20.

is, and whatever sanctions are nominally provided for, the basic sanction will be the willingness of the participants to respond vigorously, in their political and military policies, to abuses and threats of abuse. They have to be prepared to risk even the destruction of the arms agreement itself if necessary in order to deter its erosion or destruction by violations.

An important question is whether penalties and forms of redress are provided for in the agreement itself in the event of violation. To make explicit provision for exacting compensation from a violator, or to provide equivalent concessions to the victim, is to recognize that violations can occur within the agreement and that they are to be taken in stride, with countermeasures proportioned to the violations. To stipulate penalties or modes of redress may facilitate the exaction of penalties, help to eliminate further dispute over countermeasures once violations are certified, and minimize the initiative required in bringing the disputes procedure to bear. Whether or not to include such provisions should depend a good deal on whether the agreement is such that violations can occur through inadvertence, negligence, misunderstanding, unauthorized behavior, chance, *force majeure,* or excessive zeal — or could only occur through willful decision at the highest level.

As indicated earlier, the technical ramifications of a concrete arms limitation may go far beyond the level of detail that is embodied in an explicit agreement. In such circumstances, there may be good reason to deflate the significance of minor violations and to avoid the implication that a charge of violation is an accusation of bad faith. (It may be wiser to think of civil rather than criminal procedures as the analogy.) Major violations, of a kind that necessarily require policy decisions to violate, would be harder to accommodate in some "normal" disputes procedures and would raise political and diplomatic issues, whether or not a nominal procedure existed for exacting penalties. In these major cases of willful violation it would make a difference whether violations were initiated by the major powers, whose collaboration is essential to the working of the agreement, or by lesser powers that might be subjected to some kind of organized discipline.

Military Adjustment

It has to be recognized that, arms control or no arms control, the military services have their functions of defense and deterrence to perform. Even if military forces were scheduled to be reduced to zero in the process of disarmament, the important requirements of defense and of deterrence in the interim — until all potential enemies had been disarmed — would still have to be fulfilled. It is important therefore to consider the nature of the task confronting the military services, and the special problems of planning and operation that they would face.

A very substantial program of disarmament would probably confront the military services with a radical change in posture, in technology, in intelligence about the enemy, and in military responsibilities. These changes could easily require adaptations on the part of the military services just as difficult and just as extensive as those brought about by the revolutions in military technology of the last fifteen years. Strategic forces in particular would be confronted with rapidly changing requirements in a rapidly changing military environment. And there would be special problems of organization and morale in a rapidly declining force, just as there would be unprecedented requirements for cooperation and understanding between the military services and the civilian side of government.

As we indicated above the usual "indicators" of intentions and activities on the part of the potential enemy, of a kind that might constitute strategic or tactical warning, would be severely changed and disturbed or perhaps drowned out in the confusion and adaptation taking place under a severe arms-limitation process. Many sources of intelligence would become more ambiguous; and many novelties and innovations in behavior would have to be analyzed and interpreted.

Thus the dangers of misinterpreted intentions, of accidents and false alarms, of unauthorized actions and of ordinary mistakes, of unforeseen problems and difficulties, might be appreciably enhanced during the process of adopting the posture permitted under the arms-limitation agreement. And if the agreement is itself in the process of evolution, or if the agreement envisages a continuing reduction of military force or curtailment of military activity, there may be a long and dynamic period of confusion, adaptation, and of trial and error by the military services which must not only predict the usual components of the uncertain world they live in but the course of disarmament itself.

It is almost certain that important aspects of this dynamic process will have been overlooked, or mistakenly forecast, at the time the agreement was reached. Just consider, for example, a limitation on the most important means of delivery of nuclear weapons. At the present time there exists some reasonably comprehensive notion of what the significant means of delivery are. Missiles, aircraft, surface vessels, etc., within a certain range of performance, are recognized as strategically significant. But as disarmament proceeds, the defense against means of delivery may be substantially changed, the targets and the timing requirements of means of delivery would be changed, the intelligence available to both sides would be substantially changed; and radically different criteria would be required to evaluate the various modes of transportation that might qualify as militarily significant "means of delivery," together with their communication and coordination, their vulnerabilities, and their target systems.

Furthermore, there is little evidence that military research and development has yet been guided by the anticipation of severe armaments limitations resulting from negotiated arms agreements. Weapon characteristics, as they have evolved from military research and development, have on the whole not been designed for effectiveness in an arms-control environment, and have not been designed for the particular limitations on size, numbers, mode of deployment, or even the geography and communications, of a partially disarmed world.

But one must assume that if a substantial measure of arms control should be negotiated, the military services would at some stage take this into account in their research and development, their procurement, and their planning. To maximize their effectiveness under an agreement they will adapt to the limitations they can foresee; they will take advantage of the loopholes they anticipate, but will not in all cases anticipate correctly. While this process might be deplored if it led to vigorous efforts at evading the spirit of the agreement on both sides, it has to be recognized that the military services will continue to be motivated by their responsibilities for defense and deterrence, and that vigorous adaptation to the arms-control environment will be just as necessary for their *collaboration* with the arms limitations as would be required for evasion.

Just as it may be impossible to keep research and development from continually changing the technology that arms control must cope with, it would probably be naive to suppose that military plans, operations, doctrine, and attitudes, would stand still as arms limitations were imposed one after the other. Unless the initiation of arms control saps the vitality of the military services, collapses their morale, hardens their personnel policies, destroys their initiative, and freezes their technology — all of which would probably be disastrous — one must suppose that the very imposition of agreed arms limitations on the military services would stimulate radical change. And in many cases these changes would rightly prove the original arms limitations to have been inaccurate, incomplete, and in need of serious modification.

This observation has implications for the *inspection and regulation* of the arms-adjustment process. The requirements for judgment, for interpretation of facts, for difficult forecasts and projections, and the allowance for error, innovation and disorganization, will be set by the need of the regulatory process to cope with this rapidly changing military environment. And it must be able to do so without relying excessively on arbitrary and unreasonable rules and limitations, or on procedures that would destroy the respect of the military services for the rules being imposed on them in the interest of mutual security. The military services themselves must respect the purposes of arms control (even if they should disagree with them). They must respect the quality of the judgment and the decisions involved (even if they disagree with them). Their task of compliance must be made feasible; the limitations imposed on them must not seem capricious; and they must not be made to feel that those responsible for the arms controls are lacking in a sense of responsibility for the nation's security. The cooperation of the military services in an arms-control enterprise is likely to be critical to its success; and the morale and the understanding of the military services, in an arms-control environment, will still be essential to the nation's security.

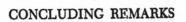

CONCLUDING REMARKS

CONCLUDING REMARKS

This has been an effort to take arms control seriously. Like any serious business, arms control is complicated and uncertain; it involves problems and risks. Like any substantially new business, it is commonly the object of oversimplification. Like any business involving the security of the nation and of the world, it gives rise to excessive hopes and naive formulations, or naive criticism and uncritical rejection. Most seriously of all, there is a tendency to think of "arms control" as a well-defined subject, one whose nature we perceive and understand, and one that stands in rather clear antithesis to the world that obtains, a world alleged to be without arms control.

We have attempted to show that arms control is a rich and variegated subject whose forms and whose impact on security policy and world affairs have been only dimly perceived. It can be as formal as a multilateral treaty or as informal as a shared recognition that certain forms of self-control will be reciprocated. It may involve some "cops and robbers" activities like cheating and detection, but may also involve many of the continuing regulatory and negotiatory processes that we associate with bureaucracy and diplomacy. It may involve the straightforward elimination of armaments or rather subtle changes in the character of armaments — even improvements in certain kinds of arms — or may involve communications, traffic rules, or other arrangements superimposed on existing military establishments. It may be as "political" as the demilitarization of a disputed country, or as little political as an understanding about noninterference in each other's military communications. And, like many reciprocal restraints that we take for granted, arms limitations may exist without our being actively aware of them.

What we have tried to emphasize more than anything else is that arms control, if properly conceived, is not necessarily hostile to, or incompatible with, or an alternative to, a military policy properly conceived. The view we have taken is that arms control is essen-

141

tially a means of supplementing unilateral military strategy by some kind of collaboration with the countries that are potential enemies. The aims of arms control and the aims of a national military strategy should be substantially the same. Before one considers this an excessively narrow construction of arms control, he should consider whether it cannot just as well be viewed as a very broad statement of what the aims of military strategy should be.

Surely arms control has no monopoly of interest in the avoidance of accidental war; anyone concerned with military policy must be concerned to minimize the danger of accident, false alarm, unauthorized action, or misunderstanding, that might lead to war. Arms control has no monopoly of interest in reducing the destructiveness of war if war occurs; military policy, too, should be concerned with the survival and welfare of the nation. Arms control need have no monopoly of virtue, in being less concerned with the nation and more concerned with humanity; a responsible military policy should not, and certainly would not, value at zero the lives and welfare of other populations, even enemy populations.

Military strategy is no longer concerned with simply the conduct of a war that has already started towards some termination that is taken for granted. Especially since World War II, military strategy has been as concerned with *influencing* potential enemies as with defeating them in combat. The concept of "deterrence" is itself a recognition that certain outcomes are worse for both ourselves and our potential enemies than other outcomes, and that a persuasive threat of military action coupled with a promise to withhold such action if the other country complies may be more significant than the military action itself. The concept of limited war is a recognition that we and our potential enemies may have a common interest, even after war starts, in limiting our objectives and checking war. Thus, military policy itself recognizes that we have a common interest with our potential enemies in avoiding a mutually destructive war, and a common interest in limiting war even if it occurs.

But sophistication comes slowly. Military collaboration with potential enemies is not a concept that comes naturally. Tradition is against it.

What we call "arms control" is really an effort to take a long overdue step towards recognizing the role of military force in the modern world. The military and diplomatic worlds have been kept unnaturally apart for so long that their separation came to seem natural. Arms control is a recognition that nearly all serious diplomacy involves sanctions, coercion and assurances involving some kind of power or force, and that a main function of military force is to influence the behavior of other countries, not simply to spend itself in their destruction.

It is the conservatism of military policy that has caused "arms control" to appear as an alternative, even antithetical, field of action. Perhaps arms control will eventually be viewed as a step in the assimilation of military policy in the over-all national strategy — as a recognition that military postures, being to a large extent a response to the military forces that oppose them, can be subject to mutual accommodation. Adjustments in military postures and doctrines that induce reciprocal adjustments by a potential opponent can be of mutual benefit if they reduce the danger of a war that neither side wants, or contain its violence, or otherwise serve the security of the nation.

This is what we mean by arms control.

APPENDIX

PARTICIPANTS AND VISITORS, THE SUMMER STUDY ON ARMS CONTROL

Sidney S. Alexander
Industrial Management, M.I.T.
Arthur Barber
Sperry Rand Corporation
Sudbury, Massachusetts
Hans A. Bethe
Laboratory of Nuclear Studies
Cornell Univ.
George F. Bing
Lawrence Radiation Laboratories
Livermore, California
Lincoln P. Bloomfield
Center for International Studies
M.I.T.
Lewis C. Bohn
Systems Research Center
Lockheed Aircraft Corp.
Frank E. Bothwell
Director, Laboratories for
Applied Sciences
Univ. of Chicago
Donald G. Brennan
Lincoln Laboratory, M.I.T.
George F. Brewer
Asst. Executive Officer, American
Academy of Arts and Sciences
Thomas Brewer
M.I.T.
David F. Cavers
Harvard Univ. Law School
H. Roberts Coward
Political Science Section, M.I.T.
Robert Donohue
Advanced Research Projects
Agency
Washington, D.C.
Paul M. Doty
Department of Chemistry,
Harvard Univ.

John T. Edsall
Department of Biology,
Harvard Univ.
Bernard T. Feld
Department of Physics, M.I.T.
George Fischer
Political Science Department,
Brandeis Univ.
Roger Fisher
Harvard Univ. Law School
Raymond Foye
Mershon National Security
Program
Ohio State University
David H. Frisch
Department of Physics, M.I.T.
Marvin H. Gewirtz
New York University
Marvin Gore
Institute for Defense Analysis
Washington, D.C.
Milton Greenblatt
Massachusetts Mental Health
Center
Boston, Massachusetts
Arthur T. Hadley
Author
New York City
Morton H. Halperin
Center for International Affairs,
Harvard Univ.
Roland Herbst
Lawrence Radiation Laboratories
Livermore, California
Nancy Hoepli
Research Associate
New York City
Herman Kahn
RAND Corporation
Santa Monica, California

147

Marvin I. Kalkstein
  Air Force Cambridge Research
    Laboratories
  Bedford, Massachusetts
E. L. Katzenbach
  Air Force Cambridge Research
    Laboratories
  Bedford, Massachusetts
Dalimil Kybal
  Lockheed Aircraft Corporation
  Sunnyvale, California
Ralph Lapp
  Consultant
  Alexandria, Virginia
Leon Lederman
  Department of Physics,
    Columbia Univ.
Herbert Liederman
  Massachusetts Mental Health
    Center
  Boston, Massachusetts
R. Duncan Luce
  Department of Psychology,
    Univ. of Pennsylvania
Seymour Melman
  Graduate School of Business
    Columbia Univ.
Donald N. Michael
  The Brookings Institution
  Washington, D.C.
Thomas W. Milburn
  United States Naval Ordnance
    Test Station
  China Lake, California
Max F. Millikan
  Department of Economics;
    Director Center for
    International Studies, M.I.T.
John Mullen
  Air Force Cambridge Research
    Laboratories
  Bedford, Massachusetts
Philip Noel-Baker
  M.P., House of Commons
  London
Jay Orear
  Professor of Physics, Cornell
    Univ.

Thomas O'Sullivan
  ITEK Corporation
  Waltham, Massachusetts
John B. Phelps
  Department of Physics; Mershon
    National Security Program,
    Ohio State Univ.
Ithiel D. Pool
  Department of Economics;
    Center for International
    Studies, M.I.T.
Garry L. Quinn
  Atomic Energy Commission
  Washington, D.C.
Henry Rowen
  Center for International Affairs,
    Harvard Univ.
Joseph Salerno
  Lincoln Laboratory, M.I.T.
Edward Salpeter
  Department of Physics,
    Cornell Univ.
Miriam Salpeter
  Cornell Univ.
Thomas C. Schelling
  Professor of Economics;
    Center for International Affairs,
    Harvard Univ.
Max Singer
  Lawyer
  Washington, D.C.
Winthrop W. Smith
  Research Asst., M.I.T.
Arthur Smithies
  Department of Economics,
    Harvard Univ.
Louis D. Smullin
  Elec. Engineering, M.I.T.
Louis B. Sohn
  Harvard Univ. Law School
Victor F. Weisskopf
  Department of Physics, M.I.T.
Jerome B. Wiesner
  Elec. Engineering; Director,
    Research Laboratory of
    Electronics, M.I.T.

Printed in September 2021
by Rotomail Italia S.p.A., Vignate (MI) - Italy